CHARISMA BASED LEADERSHIP

CHARISMA BASED LEADERSHIP

HOW TO BE THE LEADER THAT EVERYONE WANTS TO FOLLOW

LARRY COLE, PH.D.
BYRD BAGGETT, CSP

TURNER

Turner Publishing Company

445 Park Avenue, 9th Floor
New York, NY 10022
Phone: (646)291-8961   Fax: (646)291-8962

200 4th Avenue North, Suite 950
Nashville, TN 37219
Phone: (615)255-2665   Fax: (615)255-5081

Charisma-Based Leadership:
How to Be the Leader That Everyone Wants to Follow

www.turnerpublishing.com

Cover design by Mike Penticost

Library of Congress Cataloging-in-Publication Data

Baggett, Byrd.
Charisma-based leadership : how to be the leader that everyone wants to follow /
Byrd Baggett & Larry Cole.
    p. cm.
ISBN 978-1-59652-793-5
1. Leadership. 2. Leadership--Psychological aspects. I. Cole, Larry, 1945- II.
Title.
HD57.7.B336 2011
658.4'092--dc22

2010051130

Printed in the United States of America

11 12 13 14 15 16 17 18 — 0 9 8 7 6 5 4 3 2 1

To the many client friends who have entrusted us
to serve their organizations.

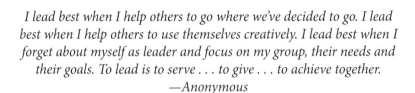

I lead best when I help others to go where we've decided to go. I lead best when I help others to use themselves creatively. I lead best when I forget about myself as leader and focus on my group, their needs and their goals. To lead is to serve . . . to give . . . to achieve together.
—*Anonymous*

Contents

Acknowledgments

I want to thank the authors of the many books that I have read who emphasized the importance of creating a personal mission statement. I heeded their advice in 1988 and simply wrote that mine was "To help people." In 1989, I founded my consulting company and give credit to my personal mission statement for a successful career as a consultant, author, and speaker. Knowing that I was living my purpose in life helped me weather some very difficult and challenging storms.

I also want to thank the thousands of employees that I have had the pleasure to work with for challenging and pushing me. These employees helped me develop much of the content you are reading in this book, and I have been applying this information for over fifteen years.

Finally, I want to thank my coauthor, Byrd Baggett. A

mutual acquaintance introduced us several years ago, and immediately we became friends and business associates. Both of us believe that there are no coincidences. Byrd is the creative one in this working relationship. He is known for creating quotes and acronyms. His creativity is responsible for fourteen books. Byrd, I thank you for your friendship and for being a trusted business associate.

—Larry Cole

This book is dedicated to the most influential man in my life, Byrd Baggett, Jr. He's not only my father but he's my best friend and hero. He's a simple man who taught me the power of grace and gratitude. I will never forget his answer to my question, "Dad, why have you always been happy?" "Bubba, I just think God put me here to serve others." I think my Dad's words capture it all. If you desire to become an authentic leader whom people want to follow, focus on becoming a part of something greater than self. If you make that one commitment, you'll make the world a better place.

—Byrd B. "Bubba" Baggett III

A special thanks to Christina Huffines with Turner Publishing for her professional assistance in bringing this book to life. We are so grateful for her patience, expertise, and wonderful attitude.

Introduction

"The essence of leadership is building relationships that stand the tests of time and change."

Welcome and thank you for reading *Charisma-Based Leadership: How to Be the Leader That Everyone Wants to Follow.* Our goal is to introduce leadership qualities and characteristics that will have a positive impact on those who follow you. It's an easy-to-read book you'll want to keep on your desk to use as a reference.

We use the analogy of train tracks throughout the book to emphasize the importance of people and leadership within an organization. The railroad company maintains both rails so the train successfully reaches its destination. Similarly, your organization has two rails: the technical rail and the people rail. Like the railroad, both rails must be well maintained for your organization to be financially successful.

If your organization is like most, the technical rail receives the bulk of attention for many reasons. First, the technical side is traditionally viewed as being the profit generator for the company. Second, the technical rail is much easier to work with than the people track. Third, managers don't know how to work with the people rail in spite of the fact that people create most of their problems. Fourth, managers have very little control over how people decide to behave. Fifth, the performance standards for the people rail are typically not defined as they are for the technical rail. Sixth is the belief that you can't teach effective interpersonal skills, so you hire for attitude and teach technical skills. In reality, it's not that people can't learn more effective interpersonal skills—leaders don't know how to teach interpersonal skills. Last of all, organizations have wasted training dollars on seminars to improve people skills without seeing changes in performance. Again, the blame is placed on the seminar participants or the seminar leader when it's really the organization to blame for not establishing a system to help drive the behavior changes.

Having said all of that, what do you have without people in the organization? Nothing. Who are the real money generators in your company? People working with people. What is the number-one reason your valuable talent walks out the door? People problems with their supervisors. What is the number-one reason employees are asked to leave the company? Their inability to work with people. Improving organizational performance occurs only when people change first. Your organization is all about people. That speaks to the fact that the people track should receive as much attention as the technical track.

As a leader, you are expected to have a reasonable amount of technical expertise and product knowledge in your field. You also need to know how to work with people. That is the very reason this book is so important for you.

Section One introduces critical product knowledge, beginning with showing you how to manage the energy systems inherent in the change process to help you lead change, improve your interpersonal performance, and coach others to do the same. We've included a personal change system to make the change process easier for you. In Section Two you will learn twelve leadership principles that will help you set the stage to work people smart—that is, to work more effectively with people. Section Three provides behavioral performance standards for ten critical leadership and workplace values. We're giving you a behavioral blueprint to make these values come alive in your workplace by removing the "I don't know how" excuse to create an environment characterized by trust, respect, teamwork, open communication, and more. You can have as much of these critical resources as you want by following the provided behavioral blueprints. The focus of Section Four is to provide you with the blueprint to work more successfully with different personalities and with conflict. Section Five discusses other critical leadership requirements—knowing your purpose, following your passion, being resilient, and controlling your ego. Section Six introduces additional leadership ideas that you'll find extremely beneficial as you continue your journey to improve your leadership effectiveness.

We hope you enjoy reading this book as much as we've enjoyed making the content of this book available to you.

Section One
Leading Change

"The winds of change will blow you away or take you to new heights."

Change is such a perplexing subject. It is "the one constant in the world." (It would be nice to receive a dollar
for every time we've heard that.) Even more perplexing is
that change is responsible for your organization's financial
success as well as your personal success. As Byrd points out,
"You're either green and growing or ripe and rotting." There
is no status quo. The dynamic laws of nature simply don't allow it. Think about that for a minute. Everything deteriorates
without use. Your body is an excellent example. Effort is

required to keep you in good physical shape. What happens when you stop your physical exercise routine? Your body quickly deteriorates.

The change subject becomes even more complicated. As a leader, you are responsible for both selling ideas of change as well as implementing them. The strategy typically employed when implementing technical change is rather simple and straightforward. Someone decides what or how the technical systems are being changed, and then people are told or trained on how to implement the change. The change template is literally forced onto the organization, demanding that people change or else.

Implementing change to improve people skills, namely teamwork and leadership effectiveness, is even more challenging. You don't have the same degree of control with these changes as you do technical ones. People have choices, and each person decides the degree to which they will implement the desired changes necessary to improve their skills. This is why many authors state that billions of dollars are wasted training people skills, because there is little, if any, follow-up. That is, subsequent to the training event designed to improve interpersonal performance, the participants return to their comfort zone—organizational culture—and it's business as usual.

This is why we propose that (1) systems must drive behavior change, and (2) transfer of training must be measured.

You would think that with our capability to think, reason, and make decisions that we would be better than a simple rubber band. Yet the similarity is so striking that it's scary. If you stretch a rubber band and want it to remain stretched, you must have a system in place to do so. Remove the system and it returns to its original state. The identical deterioration process occurs when we ask people to change. Unless there is a system in place, rapid deterioration occurs. What happens to safety or quality issues if you remove the systems underwriting the success of these two variables? Exactly, both deteriorate. Thus, you hold people accountable to implement *the systems* driving the success of both of these crucial variables.

We wish the same degree of accountability were available when implementing change on the people side of the business. Without going into detail, we rely on measuring people skills as an accountability tool in a manner similar to using numbers to improve technical performance. To learn more about this process, visit www.teammax.net.

Here's another interesting phenomenon. You've got a cemetery behind your building labeled "the idea of the month." It's estimated that 70 percent of organizational change efforts fail and are buried in this cemetery. A major contributor to these premature deaths is the inability to manage the change systems inherent in the change process. It's impossible to determine the potential progress lost because excellent ideas were buried.

You would think that in view of the importance of change to our organizational and personal successes that this would be one of the first developmental topics offered by your organization. How many training sessions have you attended that speak to the importance of you changing your behavior without them addressing the topic of how to change your behavior? Without naming names, we could list several major training companies that don't even have this subject listed as one of their courses. Now does that make any sense?

Because this book is about change and improving your leadership effectiveness, it is fitting that we remove the mystery for you at the beginning. This section is devoted to showing you a seven-step systemic process to successfully manage the energies associated with change. Think about that, energies are either driving change or working to keep you in the comfort zone. The stronger of these energy sources often wins. Since systems drive behavior changes, we're going to show you how to manipulate these energy systems to improve your success rate. By reading this section, you will never have to use the "I don't know how to change" excuse again. As you read this section, note that the required seven steps occur in sequence.

Step One:

Accepting Responsibility

"He didn't get promoted, blamed it on his luck; the office gossip was he likes to pass the buck." —Cecil Baxter

Would life be easier if you could blame other people and events for your actions? The victim mentality can be used as an excuse for irrational behavior and not achieving goals because it removes the responsibility that you did or did not do something to control your destiny. Larry was coaching a VP of manufacturing who had a history of emotional outbursts. The VP never accepted responsibility for his behavior, blaming his DNA and tendency to act just like his mother.

Kerry Patterson, Joseph Grenny, Ron McMillan, and Al Switzler offer the following illustration in their best-selling book *Crucial Conversations: Tools for Talking When Stakes Are High* to explain the fact that we automatically apply our personal meaning to experiences, which can lead to erroneous interpretations.

Experience > Story > Feelings > Actions

Upon experiencing an event, you automatically interpret and apply your reality to that event, thereby creating feelings that lead to behaviors. The interpretation can occur so quickly that you're not aware of it, but the sequence takes place nevertheless. Your imagination generates the interpretation based on what you "think" happened. Thus, it's possible that your imagination-generated story may not be based on facts, but the interpretation still generates feelings and actions. In other words, don't always believe what you think.

In order for you to improve your leadership performance, it is imperative that you accept the reality that you're in control of your story and therefore your behavior. You can't always control what happens to you, but you can control your reactions to what happens to you. The key is to acquire the necessary self-discipline and self-control to ensure that your actions maximize your effectiveness.

The degree to which you believe your story, and thus your behavior, are controlled by external events can lead to victim mentality, rendering you helpless to become an effective leader. Think about that for a moment. Do you believe those external events that you think control you will maximize your potential as a leader? No. You are in control of your destiny. Larry was told by his high school superintendent that he did not have the necessary intelligence to be a successful college student. If he had believed that superintendent, he would not have coauthored this book.

Yes, you are a product of your DNA and learning history, and these will influence your decisions. But history doesn't have to predict your present. The decisions you make today influence but don't determine the person you become tomorrow. Tomorrow you make decisions in terms of how you act today.

In preparation for the next step in your personal change sequence, please answer the following questions. Remember, honesty is always the best policy.

Accepting Responsibility Exercise

Question	Yes	No
Do I accept the brutal truth about what I am doing to facilitate as well as interfere with teamwork?		
Can I control my behavior?		
Can I change my behavior?		
Am I willing to learn how to manage change to improve my performance?		

Am I willing to experience whatever discomfort is associated with change to improve my effectiveness?		
Do I accept the responsibility to improve my performance?		
Do I want to add value in my interactions with others?		
Do I want to maximize my leadership effectiveness?		
Do I seek feedback about how I am perceived by those with whom I work?		

If the "no" column is filled with check marks, then you need to seriously question your readiness to move forward. In this instance, we recommend that you discuss these results with your supervisor or personal coach.

Otherwise, let's assume that you filled each column with "yes." Now you're ready to move to the next step in the change process.

Step Two:

Recognize the Need to Change

"There is danger in the comfort zone."

Y ou are ready to change when you accept that staying "as is" is not an option. One method of making changes is to create a personal epidemic of frustration for the particular leadership behavior that needs strengthening. That is, you must think about the frustrations and disappointments that your "as is" behavior is causing you. That frustration must be a powerful force to push you out of your comfort zone. For example, Larry's introversion interfered with his being an effective teacher. The first class he taught as a graduate student was for fellow graduate students. This shy, introverted graduate student was an intimidated, terrified, terrible instructor. Most of the students were doctoral candidates, and he hadn't even obtained his master's degree yet. Fortunately, he lived through that ordeal. Upon being asked to teach an off-campus class the next semester, he decided that something had to change. He could not continue teaching like he did the previous semester.

The following figure presents an illustration of the energy inherent in Step Two. Note the greater number of minuses than pluses, which represent the propulsion associated with the frustrations to push you out of your comfort zone.

Recognizing the Need

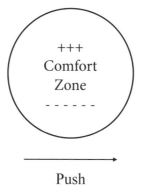

Push

We recommend that you generate a list of the advantages and disadvantages of staying "as is," because that process will help you see and accept "ownership." Like the tremendous thrust required to get the spaceship's deadweight off the launching pad, a tremendous thrust can be necessary to move you off your launching pad.

Recognizing the need to change is often easier on the technical side of the business than with the personal improvement side. If production is at only 70 percent capacity, the need to change is obvious. Recognizing that your leadership behaviors are only 70 percent effective is not as obvious. There are numerous assessments that measure specific leadership characteristics and can show a performance gap between your score and a statistical norm. You can even use such assessments in a multi-rater environment.

Data are also important to help you recognize the need to change. The popular 360° assessment is used to quantify perceptions to identify behaviors that need strengthening in order to improve leadership effectiveness. Overall, however, establishing performance standards for leadership effectiveness and measuring performance with these standards is challenging and frequently not attempted. We address the issue of leadership performance standards in Section 3.

Larry is working with a mid-level manager to improve the working relationships with his team members. Two steps had to occur before the manager accepted the need to change. First, a focus group with a sample of team members listed the specific behaviors the manager exhibited to create the perception that he didn't care for team members as individuals or was not interested in their input. Second, his vice-president made it very clear that the manager's job security in his present position required him to improve leadership effectiveness. Sometimes, very dire circumstances must occur as a wake-up call to grab your attention. We hope that's not the case with you.

Imagine for a moment that you're in a movie theater. Suddenly, the theater goes completely dark, including the emergency exits. Immediately, the moviegoers begin coughing due to an accumulation of smoke. Do you think the crowd will exhibit frustration? Do you think they will move to action? Without clear direction as to how to exit the theater, the panic can be harmful. How would the scene change with the exits clearly marked? Knowing the location of the exits speaks to the critical need of knowing the desired behaviors that are detailed in Step Three of the seven-step change process.

Step Three:

Know the Desired Behaviors

"Behavior is what a man does, not what he thinks, feels, or believes."

—*Emily Dickinson*

Step Three sounds easy, but it may be more challenging than you think. What if you decide that you want to be friendlier, more approachable, more humble, or the person your team members will feel free to tell anything to? These are crucial leadership behaviors. Specifically, what behaviors need to be learned or strengthened? You don't just become more approachable. You must practice specific behaviors that tell others that they can interact with you.

The challenge with people skills is their abstraction, which makes them difficult to define. For a moment, consider the relatively simple act of being friendly. Ask ten people the specific behaviors needed to be friendly, and you can get ten different answers. That can be confusing.

- To change your behavior, you must:
- Know what you want to achieve.
- Have a road map to get where you want to go.
- Use a system to help you bring about the desired behavior change.
- Use feedback (i.e., data) as a guide to becoming happier.

For example, suppose you want to be the person people feel free to communicate with—the behavior you want to achieve. You're not going to just be that person; you must interact with your team members very specifically to send the message that each can communicate to you without fear. What behaviors do you need to exhibit so people feel safe? This road map may include the following behaviors:

1. Structure input into decisions that affect others.
2. Constantly ask others for their suggestions on how you can improve with an open-ended question: "What can be done to improve?"
3. Use the input offered by others whenever possible.
4. Publicly recognize the benefits derived from ideas

contributed by others.

5. Use mistakes as learning opportunities.

6. Remain emotionally calm, especially when being told about mistakes, frustrations, and other disappointments.

As a sidebar, Larry jokingly tells audiences about a time a wife asked her husband if he thought the blouse she had on looked good with the pants she was wearing. He thought she had a blouse that would look a little better and indicated so in a socially appropriate manner. You know the rest of that story. Now when asked that same question, he always tells her that she looks good in whatever she's wearing. The point is, you can quickly shut people down and create an environment of fear.

Note that the six behaviors listed in the above example are specific and empirical, which allows you to model them and allows your team members to see them. Consequently, they can be taught, repeated, and their use measured. Also, we must emphasize the importance of writing the desired behaviors in terms of what you want to do instead of what you don't want to do. When you're "not" doing something, you're substituting a behavior "to do" something. Speak in terms of where you are going, and that increases the likelihood of you getting there.

In Section Three, you will learn the specific leadership behaviors of an authentic leader that results in a high-performing workplace, achieved by engaging and developing people. In alignment with Step Three, you will learn the specific leadership values and behaviors that make each come alive.

At this point, you should understand the importance of knowing where you want to go and the need for a behavioral blueprint.

Step Four:

Be Willing to Change

"You must let go to grow."

You control the personal motivation to be your best version of an authentic leader. First is the degree of intensity manifested in Step Two. That is, there is a positive correlation between the intensity level of exclaiming that remaining "as is" is not an option and your personal motivation to change. That is the reason we encouraged you to create an epidemic of frustration associated with the disadvantages of your current situation. The second piece of your personal motivation puzzle is the intensity of the magnetic quality you create.

Remember an instance of purchasing an item that exceeded your budget? The excitement associated with the purchase literally pulled money right out of your pocket. The magnetic quality of that item helped you make the decision, "I must do whatever is necessary to purchase this item." You want the identical force operating to increase your willingness to change. The advantages associated with the desired behavior listed in Step Three create the pull. A positive correlation exists between these advantages and the degree to which you're willing to change.

In the following figure, which pertains to the new behavior, note that the pluses outnumber the minuses. This illustrates the intensity of the advantages of the new behavior. Because the act of writing increases the intensity of this crucial energy source, we encourage you to record the advantages and disadvantages of the desired behavior.

Willing to Change

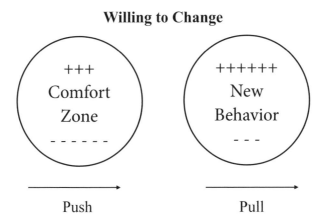

The figure illustrates the two energy sources that you manipulate to increase your willingness to change. If these were the only energy sources, change would be easy. Unfortunately, that's not the case; you'll learn about other energy sources in Step Six. But first, we must discuss a crucial step of the change process that is often overlooked.

Step Five
See Yourself Doing the Desired Behavior

"Wisdom is knowing what to do next; virtue is doing it."

—David Starr Jordan

Your body follows what you see yourself doing. For example, Larry has never touched a snake, let alone pick one up! He has no intention of doing so either because he simply does not see himself doing that.

The important point is you must see yourself using the behaviors listed in Step Three. This visualization concept is easily demonstrated in a classroom environment. Tell students to imagine a two-by-twelve-inch board, twenty-five feet in length, lying flat on the floor. Offer each student

$100 for walking on this board without their feet touching the floor. You'll give away as many $100 bills as there are students in the class. Now ask them to imagine the board has been raised to ten feet. How many people would walk the board without a safety rope or net? Do the same with the board at twenty-five feet and then fifty feet, and you'll see the number of willing participants drop as the height increases. The reason is that people begin seeing themselves fall, and that negative vision prevents them from taking the risk of walking the board.

Golfers know the reality of vision all too well. Ask golfers what club they would use to hit to a 165 yard par three hole. Then tell them the rest of the story—there are 150 yards of water between the tee box and the green. Repeat the question, "What club would you use?" Many golfers will change clubs and get a water ball out of their bag. They see the ball going into the water, which increases the likelihood of it happening. The psychology of golf is seeing where you want the ball to go. In this case, water is taken out of play as the golfer focuses on hitting the green.

The impact of your personal vision reinforces the importance of writing a positive description for the desired behavior that was listed in Step Three. That is, it is very difficult to see yourself not doing something as opposed to doing something. For example, what do you see when you see yourself not getting emotionally upset? Contrast the image you're trying to create with one of remaining emotionally calm. You get the point.

Now you're ready to change. You've completed the first five steps to get to this point—changing. Now the real work begins.

Step Six:

Change

"To truly change, one must embrace the pain of discipline."

Congratulations, you've completed the first five steps to get to the point at which you can begin to change. As you are about to learn, the preparatory work is extremely beneficial for the success of your long-term changes. The excitement you generated from Step Two and Step Four are about to hit a brick wall labeled *resistance.* Most people consider resistance as negative. Our intent is to create a paradigm shift that will help you see resistance as inherently positive.

We've got a lot to discuss in Step Six. Let's begin by showing you the remaining energy sources inherent in the change process. We've expanded the previous two figures to show the association with Steps Two and Four. As you examine the following figure, you will see that we've added several sources of resistance. Note that the arrows encouraging change are dashed, signifying they've lost intensity in view of the resistance. We're going to describe the resistance and then address what you must do to override the temptation to quit.

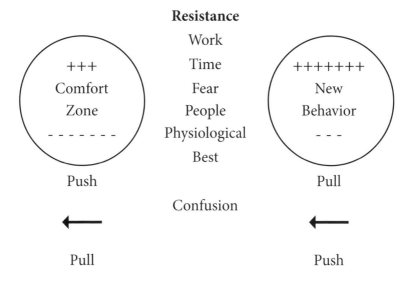

- **Work** is required for you to substitute the desired behavior for the undesired one.
- **Time** is required to make changes. In his book *Talent is Overrated: What Really Separates World-Class Performers from Everybody Else*, Geoff Colvin points out that world-class performers practice for at

least 10,000 hours, accumulated over time. Practice is serious business for these elite performers. Each session is focused to improve a specific element of performance with the expectation to be better at the end of the practice than the start. According to the 10,000 hour rule, if you use every hour of the workday in focused practice, you can become a world-class performer in a matter of five years.

- *Fear* is generated to the extent that you step out of the comfort zone to improve your leadership effectiveness. The greater your perceived risk, the greater the fear.

- There may be *people* who prefer that you don't change.

- Research shows a *physiological* basis for resistance. That is, established neurological pathways guide behaviors. When the brain detects that you're doing something out of the ordinary, it automatically goes into protection mode to fight-or-flight. Thus, change requires building a new neurological highway to support the new behavior. That requires *time* and *work.*

- Through it all, you might even wonder if the change is best for you. You might try to rationalize, I have been successful, so why put myself through the effort and discomfort to improve my performance?

- The combination of the above resistance factors generates considerable forces that encourage you to take the path of least resistance and return to the comfort zone. You've got to have the discipline to avoid the temptation of returning to the comfort zone. As illustrated in the figure, the sources encouraging you to change versus those encouraging you to remain the same create considerable confusion.

The desire of your body to stay in a state of balance or to be tension-free adds another level of complexity to the situation. Change produces tension. This tension triggers your mind to believe that something is wrong; thus, your body wants to protect itself by removing this foreign substance. There are two ways to rid your body of the tension created by resistance: grow through the resistance, or take the path of least resistance and quit. To continue the journey to change, you want to use resistance as your friend and entice your creative mind to continue generating ideas. Using resistance as your friend is not an oxymoron. Consider the positive elements associated with resistance. First, your body is telling you that you're changing, which is exactly what you want to do. Second, by continuing to accept the resistance, your mind operates according to a psychological principle called the Law of Closure. This process will likewise serve as your friend and create ideas for you to continue to achieve the desired behavior listed in Step Three. Third, you improve your skill set to work with resistance. By doing so, adapting to change in the future will become easier and more natural.

It's time to introduce our signature lesson from Mother Nature. For just a moment, contrast the journey of a turtle and squirrel as each crosses a road. While the turtle is crossing, it withdraws into its shell—or comfort zone—upon hearing the car. When the fear subsides, it sticks its neck from its comfort zone and continues on the journey. The squirrel, on the other hand, becomes temporarily paralyzed when it sees the car. It ultimately decides to return to its comfort zone along the side of the road. You know how that story most often ends—the squeal of tires, and attempting to return to the comfort zone claims another victim! If it had been smart like the turtle and had taken its comfort zone with it, it would have been safe, as most drivers try to avoid hitting the turtle or squirrel.

During the trying times of change, most people tend to be a squirrel. As a leader, you've got to be a turtle and take your comfort zone with you. You can stop and re-group like the turtle when the going gets tough, but eventually, you must continue on the change journey.

As explained earlier, Larry has never touched a snake and has no plans to do so. But should he plan to, he would have to face his fear and touch one. The second time would be easier than the first, the third easier than the second, and so on. Facing resistance and then changing is the only way to acquire self-confidence. Therefore, the fourth advantage of working with resistance is gaining self-confidence.

Step Six speaks to the heart and soul of your personal change process. The rubber band phenomenon illustrates how crucial it is for you to change. What happens when you stretch a rubber band and then release it? It returns to its original shape, just like you want to return to your comfort zone. You must employ a system to keep the rubber band stretched. You're stretched like the rubber band as you step out of the comfort zone to grow. Using a system helps you to be like the turtle and continue to grow through inevitable resistance. The remainder of this chapter details that system.

Personal Change System

The first step in this system of growth is to recognize that you're practicing leadership skills all day. The choice you must make is which set of skills will you continue to practice—those that enhance your leadership effectiveness, or those that sabotage your leadership? Obviously, you want to choose to practice the most effective skills.

Next, schedule two special practice sessions. The first is practicing through visualization. That is, you can visualize exercising the desired behavior listed in Step Three. The second is practicing through a role-playing session in a classroom environment or with a colleague or coach. The more frequently you practice, the faster you change.

Now let's put a personal change system to work. The objective of the system is to saturate your day with a focus to change.

1. Put in writing the advantages and disadvantages of the behavior you want to change (Step Two), the person you want to become (Step Three), and the advantages and disadvantages of the desired behavior

(Step Four). As mentioned, the physical act of writing encourages ownership.

2. In the words of Stephen Covey, "begin with the end in mind." Start each day thinking about and visualizing the person you want to become.

3. Put your top ten blessings in writing and review these at the beginning of each day. Doing so reminds you that life is a blessing and gives you a psychological boost.

4. List your major achievements and review these each morning. Doing so provides the same psychological boost that occurs when you review your blessings. (Some days you may need all the psychological energy you can muster!)

5. Set aside specific times in your daily schedule to visualize using the desired behaviors.

6. Take advantage of repeating a positive affirmation throughout the day.

7. At the end of the day, evaluate your performance while focusing on the successes experienced during the day. Some days you're going to blow it. Admit doing so and commit to making tomorrow a more successful day.

8. The challenge is to exert the necessary self-discipline to control you at those inevitable times you're tempted to regress. The Stop & Think technique, developed by psychologists George Batsche and Howard Knoff, helps you acquire the necessary self-

control. You know when the temptation to return to the comfort zone strikes. At that precise moment, tell yourself to stop and think. Ask, "Do I want to make a good choice or a bad choice?" Psychologically, the answer is obvious. If you need to, review the disadvantages from Step Two that give you the push to change, and the advantages from Step Four that provide the strong magnetic pull to change. Then make the decision to avoid the temptation to return to the comfort zone (remember the fate of the squirrel), and instead, like the turtle, continue on your change journey.

During the more challenging times of the change process, you can continue to manage your personal motivation. Revisit the disadvantages of the old behavior that pushed you to state, "Remaining 'as is' is not an option," and the advantages of the new behavior which pulled you to state, "I've got to be that person." Of these two, the pull of the new behavior is crucial to success. It is imperative to keep your eyes locked on the person you want to be. Doing so continues to provide hope, which in turn provides the energy to walk through the struggles of change. Norman Vincent Peale said it best: "You quit only when you accept the image of defeat."

Step Seven
Feedback

"Feedback is the breakfast of champions." —*Ken Blanchard, author and management expert*

It's easy to forget about the importance of feedback. Feedback allows you to do everything you do, but we just expect our bodies to continue this valuable function while we take it for granted. About the only time the importance of feedback is recognized is when you're lost; the feedback you previously received doesn't make sense anymore, often resulting in confusion and frustration.

Feedback is crucial to the change formula because it is required for long-term behavioral change. All of us have known people who have tried unsuccessfully to change a bad habit. The feedback told them the pain of change was more intense than the success achieved. In this instance, the focus was placed on the frustration and lack of progress. During the change process, you want to reverse the focus and celebrate successes. The change might not happen as quickly as you would like or had expected, but keep your eyes locked on where you want to go and enjoy the successes. As Byrd states, "Don't quit before the blessing."

Here's an illustration on the use of feedback. Point a blindfolded marksman at the target and ask him to shoot at it. He might get lucky and hit the target without any feedback. (Even a blind hog finds an acorn occasionally.) Give the blindfolded marksman immediate and specific feedback, and he will hit the target within a few tries. The longer the delay between the shot and the feedback, the more difficult it will be for him to hit the target.

It's important for you to do the same—provide yourself immediate and specific feedback. Focus on your successes, because doing so provides the essential energy for you to be like the turtle to continue on your journey to success. It would be nice to receive immediate and specific positive feedback from significant people in your life, but don't depend upon it when making the necessary changes to improve your leadership skills. Unfortunately, most of us are not as proficient at providing feedback as we need to be. That's why you need to depend on yourself for the affirming feedback.

We'll close this section with a brief list of seven

habits leaders can develop to commit to change and learn from feedback. As Byrd says, "If you're not changing, you're no longer in first place."

- Competence – learn something new.
- Character – always do the right thing.
- Communication – ask the right questions.
- Compassion – make someone feel special.
- Connection – plant the seeds of relationships.
- Commitment – action changes things.
- Courage – take personal responsibility for your life.

Section Two

Twelve Leadership Principles That Create A High-Performing Workplace

Leadership

Which leader would you rather follow? A leader who creates the reputation of being confident, innovative, respectful, trusting, cooperative, and straightforward, or one who is manipulative and unethical, lacks integrity, must always be right, and allows personal agendas to take precedence over the company's agenda? Now for the pivotal question: Which of these two sets of descriptions describes you?

There are at least three very important reasons for you to answer this question. First, your leadership behaviors tell others about your values, and your values speak volumes about you as a person. Second, your behaviors send the message to your followers about what is acceptable in the organization. (Yes, your behaviors contribute to your organization's corporate culture.) Third, your behaviors contribute to the efficiency or inefficiency of your organization. Or the worst-case scenario is that your leadership behaviors can create a dysfunctional workplace of chaos and confusion.

Our research shows that people problems cost an organization up to 25 percent of its operating efficiency. Multiply that percentage times your operating budget and see if you like the numbers. The efficiency of your work unit begins with you—the leader. Your goal is to model the twelve leadership principles introduced in this section and encourage your people to do the same. Imagine the synergy created if every manager in your organization became a leader that people wanted to follow. There is no doubt that performance would dramatically improve.

Principle One
Accepting the Brutal Truth

"The truth may sometimes hurt but it will always help."

To begin, you must accept the brutal truth about your leadership behaviors. Do you want your people to accept the truth about their behaviors? Sure you do, for the obvious reason that to improve the performance and profitability of your organization requires all leaders to improve their behaviors. Examine the following figure.

Awareness and Competency

	Not Competent	*Competent*
Not Aware	Not Aware	Not Aware
	Not Competent	Competent
Aware	Aware	Aware
	Not Competent	Competent

The desired position is being acutely aware of your strengths and weaknesses. The most challenging position is being unaware of your incompetency. For a moment, consider the consequences associated with this blind spot. The ultimate consequence is that it could derail your career. Our guess is that is not your desired outcome.

What would happen if you were blind to your organization's technical incompetence? That would be an expensive blind spot that could cost your organization a lot of money in lost productivity. You certainly don't want your organization to operate at 75 percent efficiency. For the same reason, you don't want to operate at 75 percent efficiency of your leadership potential.

There are two factors that you must consider in order to maximize your leadership potential. First, become like a sponge in terms of feedback: seek, understand, and use it. There are an infinite number of sources of this valuable information. One is to constantly monitor your thoughts, feelings, and actions. What is your body telling you about you? Obtaining feedback from others is a valuable source. People can provide you either verbal feedback (more on this subject later in this section) or quantitative feedback, namely multi-rater assessments. Taking self-assessments on various leadership topics can provide valuable insight into your behaviors as well as the behaviors of others. (See Appendix for self-assessment resources.) The bottom line is that you want to learn as much about you as possible.

The second factor to be controlled is your ego. In *Egonomics: What Makes Ego Our Greatest Asset (or Most Expensive Liability),* authors David Marcum and Steven Smith state, "Often the hardest side of business to master is the human side, and nothing is more human than ego. How we manage ego on the human side affects everything we do on the business side, one way or the other." These far-reaching effects are the very reason we've emphasized controlling your ego in this book (see the chapter on Controlling the Ego).

As feedback becomes available to you, you will either:

1. Deny it.
2. Listen to it, but do nothing with it.
3. Use it to maximize your performance.

Obviously, the first two options are career-busters. Monitor your reactions and consider that the more intense your emotional reaction to not accept feedback, the greater the likelihood that the feedback might be true.

Your body operates in accordance to the pleasure-pain principle. The truth often hurts, and you must resist the temptation to push the pain aside. In reality, the most valuable feedback might be the most painful. Therefore, you must welcome the painful feedback with open arms while looking for information that will maximize your leadership potential. There is another very important principle to remember—you find what you are looking for. If you look for the good in the feedback, you will find it.

Principle Two

It Is My Responsibility to Help You Be Successful

"We will always beat Me."

Imagine the synergy created if everyone in your organization accepted this responsibility. The more people you help to succeed, the more people will be willing to help you. You receive what you share with others. We refer to this concept as the boomerang effect.

You want your people to be better than you are, as your success depends upon the performance of your direct reports. Just as cream rises to the top, the better your people perform, the easier and faster you will rise to the top.

You fulfill the responsibility to help people succeed organizationally and individually. Organizationally, you ensure that your organization's (or team's) vision and mission (or purpose) are defined, understood, and known by all. Providing your people recognition for completing their job responsibilities that lead to achieving the mission and vision creates organizational synergy. Individually, you help people succeed by ensuring they have challenging and meaningful work, are empowered to make independent decisions, and use the interpersonal skills to maximize working relationships. You also help them succeed by being available to mentor their progress.

As you continue to help your people achieve success, they in turn challenge you to continue progressing along your learning curve. This results in a win-win environment.

Another crucial stage to set is ensuring that your direct reports help each other (your internal customers) to be successful. "Your priorities are my priorities when you need my assistance" is the mantra for success. We promote this success by encouraging seminar participants to meet with their internal customers and ask two critical questions:

1. What am I or my people doing to create frustration in your life?
2. What can I or my people do to maximize our working relationship?

Then make every commitment to meet or exceed their expectations.

It is both surprising and disappointing to learn the number of leaders who haven't thought about engaging this simple teamwork process. Yet there are constant complaints about the silos constructed within the organization and, in some cases, leaders intentionally sabotaging the success of their internal customers. Talk about acting stupidly!

The bottom line is, people helping people succeed drives the success of your organization. For just a moment, visualize a spiderweb. Every part of that web is designed to maximize the spider's success. That spider can quickly travel about its web with ease. You want a corporate culture that is analogous to the spiderweb. Wherever your people go throughout the organization, you want them to experience the same level of success as that spider.

Your organization is not going to be any better than the people in it. If you were to graph the success of your team and company, you would want it to look like the following graph.

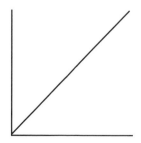

In order for that to happen, people must first improve their performance. Improved performance leads to improvement in production and profitability. Organizations change only when people change.

The weakest link determines the strength of a chain. You don't want to be that weakest link, nor do you want your people or colleagues to be the weakest link. (If it were possible to quantify the technical and people competencies of every member of your team, someone would be that weakest link.) To increase the success rate of the weakest link and therefore the entire chain, develop the reputation to competently assist as many people in your organization as possible.

Principle Three

It Is My Responsibility to Be the Person with Whom You Want to Work

"If people don't like you, they won't voluntarily follow you."

F or the most part, people don't enjoy being around horse manure because it stinks. For the same reason, they also don't enjoy being around the horse's butt. How do you think audience members answer when asked whether they know at least one "horse's butt" at work? You're right—everyone answers affirmatively. When asked whether they've been that horse's butt from time to time, again, everyone answers yes and then readily admits that people don't like working with a horse's butt. You have to wonder, then, why we sometimes act in this manner. We've listed a few reasons:

1. ***Ego.*** Unfortunately, some people think they are God's gift to mankind. Consequently, these individuals operate with the narcissistic assumption that they are too good for everyone else.

2. ***Lazy.*** Some people simply don't want to put forth the effort required to use effective interpersonal skills.

3. ***Don't care.*** Treating people like a baby treats a diaper is the norm for many individuals, and for whatever reason, they don't care to change.

4. ***Incompetent.*** Some people simply don't have the required level of competency to recognize they must be pretty good to realize they're not good enough.

5. ***Difficult to change.*** True change can be a difficult process, and these individuals prefer not to experience the degree of discomfort to do so.

6. ***Unaware of their toxicity.*** Ignorance can be bliss, but not necessarily healthy for your career. We know numerous instances of individuals who were not given feedback about the toxicity they injected into the work environment.

7. ***Do not know how to change.*** Even though change is a constant in the world, most people do not have a clue how to manage the energy systems inherent in the change process. (We eliminated this excuse with the Seven-Step Personal Change Process detailed in Section One.)

8. ***Lack emotional stability.*** Each of us has psychological quirks. It's sad to say, but some individuals have

more serious psychological issues that interfere with the use of effective interpersonal skills. If you are one of these individuals, then start working with a mental-health therapist to restore your emotional stability.

9. *Stupid.* We offer this one tongue-in-cheek. The fact is, smart people sometimes do stupid things. It does appear that many people check their common sense at the door upon entering the workplace.

Below is a self-assessment determining how you work with others. Complete the assessment honestly by using the following scale:

1 = Always Disagree	4 = Occasionally Agree
2 = Frequently Disagree	5 = Frequently Agree
3 = Occasionally Disagree	6 = Always Agree

I prefer to remain as I am rather than make the effort to improve my interpersonal skills.	1 2 3 4 5 6
People need to accept me as I am.	1 2 3 4 5 6
I prefer to not examine or admit my interpersonal ineffectiveness.	1 2 3 4 5 6
I prefer the comfort of remaining as I am rather than to experience the discomfort associated with changing my interpersonal performance.	1 2 3 4 5 6

My interpersonal skills are as good as they need to be.	1 2 3 4 5 6
I do not know how to change my interpersonal performance.	1 2 3 4 5 6
People might describe me as being egotistical.	1 2 3 4 5 6
It is extremely difficult for me to function as an effective team member.	1 2 3 4 5 6
I like being the person who creates frustration in working relationships.	1 2 3 4 5 6
People might describe me as frequently acting in stupid ways when interacting with others.	1 2 3 4 5 6

Upon completing the self-assessment, total your scores and divide by ten to calculate the mean. The preferred mean is 3 or less.

(Total) _____ ÷ 10 = _____ (Mean)

There are also many reasons you should want to be the person with whom people like to work. We've listed the critical ones.

Integrity—it's the right thing to do. Using effective interpersonal skills is just the right way to treat another human being. First, it's the kind thing to do. People deserve to be treated courteously and shown they are valued.

Second, your interpersonal behaviors are an extension of your personal values. When you treat people with disrespect, you are telling them you disregard them as fellow human beings. When you fail to do what you've agreed to do, you're telling people that you can't be trusted. Surely you want a better reputation than that.

Third, we are interdependent upon each other. Not one of us can survive without the assistance from our fellow humans. Your company's survival is dependent upon all employees working to help each other to be successful. As previously discussed, helping people become successful is your responsibility as a leader.

Fourth (also previously mentioned), leaders teach and model corporate values. As a leader, your behavior establishes the norm for your team or organization. When you openly complain about other departments, you're giving team members permission to do the same. That's not going to create a supportive teamwork environment.

Leaders frequently forget their powerful impact upon others. Testimony to this impact is that the toxic manner in which supervisors interact with their direct reports is the number-one reason employees leave their employers. The right thing to do as a supervisor is to meet the challenge to be the number-one reason valuable talent remains committed to the organization.

People power. Yes, you may have inherent power in your position and title, but real power emerges from people wanting to work with you because of the way you interact with them.

Organizational commitment. Establishing employee loyalty and retaining talent are huge challenges in today's workplace. As a leader, it is to your advantage to use the behaviors that both attract and retain talent.

Continuing personal development. We become better people as we continue to use behaviors that maximize working relationships. In his book *The Rhythm of Life: Living Every Day with Passion and Purpose,* Matthew Kelly reminds us to become the "best version of yourself." Looking at this from nature's perspective, every living entity's purpose is to be everything it can be in accordance with its genetic makeup and available nutrients. You've been powered with a brain that is a more powerful processor of information than any computer. Yet your thinking patterns can either help develop or hinder your personal development.

In relaying this fact to others, Larry often asks audiences to write down their first thought when told they can make $250,000 per year. The answers fall into one of three categories: (1) I can't, (2) Show me how, or (3) I can. He teasingly tells those who answered that they can't or those who express doubt not to spend the money yet. Henry Ford (founder of Ford Motor Company) recognized the importance of the internal environment when he stated, "Whether you think you can or think you can't, you're right."

Another point to remember about this advantage: Strive to be the employee who's too valuable to lose. You do that by continuously improving technical and interpersonal skills. Of these two skill sets, you need to know that many employers strive to hire employees with good attitudes because of the relative ease to teach the technical skills needed to competently complete job responsibilities. Additionally, employees with excellent interpersonal skills have the advantage when considered for advancement.

Easier life and more enjoyable work. Employees want to have fun at work. Laughing is nature's way of calming our bodies. It's impossible to laugh and be completely stressed out at the same time. We're not advocating that the work environment be like a comedy hour. But employees spend a significant portion of their lives in the workplace, so enjoying the work experience is conducive to good physical and emotional health. In addition, people who enjoy their work environment exhibit higher safety records as well as higher quality production. Such a work environment is a "win" for everyone. Dolly Parton once said, "When you love your work, you never go to work again."

In closing our discussion of this leadership principle, we ask you to complete the next self-assessment by using the following scale:

1 = Always Disagree	4 = Occasionally Agree
2 = Frequently Disagree	5 = Frequently Agree
3 = Occasionally Disagree	6 = Always Agree

The company's success is more important than my individual success.	1 2 3 4 5 6

I strive to use effective interpersonal skills because it is the right thing to do.	1 2 3 4 5 6
I use effective interpersonal skills to help my fellow employees to be successful.	1 2 3 4 5 6
I treat people with kindness to show that I care.	1 2 3 4 5 6
I want the reputation of using the interpersonal skills to maximize working relationships.	1 2 3 4 5 6
I use effective interpersonal skills to set an example for other employees.	1 2 3 4 5 6
I use effective interpersonal skills to encourage others to use the same with me.	1 2 3 4 5 6
I use effective interpersonal skills to encourage collaboration.	1 2 3 4 5 6
I am constantly searching to identify what I can do to improve my interpersonal effectiveness.	1 2 3 4 5 6
I use the interpersonal skills to have an enjoyable workplace.	1 2 3 4 5 6

Upon completing the self-assessment, total your scores and divide by ten to calculate the mean. The preferred mean is 5 or greater.

(Total) _____ ÷ 10 = _____ (Mean)

Log on to www.teammax.net and complete the Readiness for Change survey. Your score puts you into one of five stages of change in terms of improving your interpersonal skills in a teamwork environment. Ask your team members to do the same, and then discuss how the results impact your team.

We want to leave you with a very important question: "When you die, do you want people to come to your funeral to bid you farewell or make certain you're dead?" In Section Three, you're going to learn the behaviors to ensure that people attend your funeral to bid you farewell.

Principle Four

It Is My Responsibility to Create an Environment in Which You Feel Free to Talk to Me

"Open and honest communication is the lifeblood of growth."

Do you want people to communicate honestly with you? You probably answered in the affirmative. What if the information shared with you is critical of your performance or is in conflict with your beliefs? Would you still want the open, honest communication? We hope so, because open and honest communication is the lifeblood of trust within an organization. Communication is such an important subject that we'll revisit the topic in Section Three as a leadership value and also in Section Four when we address controlling your ego and feedback.

In *Driving Fear Out of the Workplace: Creating the
High-Trust, High-Performance Organization,* authors Kathleen Ryan and Daniel Oestreich point out that 70 percent
of employees are afraid to speak out. As you've probably
guessed, the primary root cause is fear of reprisal, namely
job security or emotional abuse. The subject most of their
research participants wanted to discuss was how badly their
supervisor treats them.

We've mentioned the influential impact you have upon
people. There are two pieces of information employees take
into consideration when deciding how honest they can be
with you. First are the verbal and nonverbal messages you
send that tell people whether they can freely talk to you or
not. The second is your reputation—what is said about your
openness to honest information. We've heard many stories
of employees expressing their opinions and then being punished for their honesty. This story about killing the messenger, whether real or perceived, will spread like a wildfire
through an organization.

You also want people to talk about how you treat them.
You want a positive reputation of others being comfortable
talking to you and telling you everything you need to know.
To develop this reputation, you must develop the habit of
asking people, "What can be done to improve . . . ?" Phrasing the question in this manner helps direct the ensuing conversation to be positive and constructive. Another option
for seeking input to challenge your thinking is to encourage
people to list the advantages and disadvantages of your idea.

If you really want to push the envelope, present the idea and ask people to tell you why it is so stupid! Their willingness to participate in that conversation will tell you volumes about their willingness to freely communicate with you.

Your reaction after listening to "bad news" is critical to helping people feel safe. Please refer to Giving Feedback and Receiving Feedback in Section Four to learn about this topic.

Principle Five
Frustration Is Your Best Friend

"My recipe for dealing with anger and frustration: set the kitchen timer for twenty minutes, cry, rant, and rave, and at the sound of the bell, simmer down and go about business as usual."

—*Phyllis Diller, comedienne*

No, this leadership principle is not an oxymoron. Before you read the title of this leadership principle, would you have said that you perceive frustrations in working relationships as a positive or a negative event?

Recently, Larry's antique pickup truck started missing out. What was that pickup telling Larry? If your automobile was about to have a major mechanical breakdown, would you prefer to know about it in advance or have it simply stop? The smart decision is to fix the problem before it gets worse.

Three working relationships determine the efficiency of your organization. The first is members of a team working together as a unit. The second is the working relationships between work units. The third is the behavioral dynamic between supervisors and their direct reports. When one person engages in a behavior that others find frustrating, the efficiency of one or more of these working relationships is disrupted immediately. People talk about the event. Production slows down or stops. Such production interruptions steal money from your financial bottom line.

Employees identify numerous frustrations in working relationships; for example, the lack of cooperation between work units, and unfair treatment. It's easy to consider venting such frustration as an enemy, but in reality, it can be a friend—a signal that some element of the working relationship needs improvement.

Using frustration as your friend requires you to override the natural pleasure-pain principle: your body prefers to avoid what's considered painful while approaching the pleasures in life. Perceiving frustration as an enemy can allow it to exist and even grow into a cancer. That's not a good thing. Speaking of frustration, Larry is reminded of working in a food processing plant and the gridlock that existed between the first-shift maintenance and production supervisors. The lack of cooperation existed for several months without intervention. You can imagine the war that created. Eventually, the parties agreed to stop using frustration as an enemy and convert it to friend status. These individuals defined and implemented teamwork strategies to help each other to be successful. The teamwork began improving immediately.

As a leader, you should identify every frustration in working relationships and use each one as an energy source to improve working relationships. Remember Step Two of the Seven-Step Personal Change Process: remaining "as is" is not an option.

Principle Six
I'm Guilty Until I Prove My Innocence

"Those who can command themselves command others."

—*William Hazlitt, English author and critic*

Effective leaders give credit to others for success achieved and take responsibility for mistakes. These leaders understand the powerful influence they have on creating a culture that maximizes working relationships and keeps employees engaged and motivated to achieve peak performance. This just seems to be the right thing to do.

How easy it is to forget that every time you point a finger at someone, there are at least three pointing back at you. Somebody is trying to send you a message. Are you listening? We're reminded of a senior manager who points fingers big time. He acts as though he's sacred. He sends blistering e-mails and is a master of emotional outrages when discussing issues with other managers. To say it's a mess is an understatement.

What is your reaction when the finger is pointing at you? Do you feel attacked, and do your survival instincts automatically work to protect you? Even when you know your actions contributed to the problem, it's easy to become defensive. When that happens, there are two resulting problems. One is the defensive emotional reaction, which only serves to escalate the initial problem. The second is the unresolved source of the original frustration. More than likely, you won't be able to resolve the original issue until the emotional reaction is defused and people feel safe.

Smart people working people smart approach the subject with the attitude of "I'm guilty." Consider your reaction when being approached by someone who asks you:

- "Do you agree there are some frustrations in the working relationship?"
- "What am I or what is my department doing that is contributing to that frustration?"
- "What can I or my department do to help you to be more successful?"

This leader not only commits to implement the changes to meet the need of their internal customer but schedules a feedback session to ensure the defined needs are met.

What would you do if that leader then asks, "Can I make a few suggestions of what you can do to help me (or us) to be more successful?"

Taking the leadership position of "guilty until proven innocent" creates a completely different psychological environment in which to solve the problem than pointing fingers does. The affected parties are much more likely to cooperate.

But remember your limitations. You can't force people to cooperate, and at times the desired cooperation won't take place. The natural temptation in this instance is to climb into the gutter with the uncooperative parties and be equally as uncooperative. Yielding to this temptation generally adds fuel to the fire, rendering you a victim controlled by the lack of cooperation. In these instances, rise above the situation and help people be successful anyway.

The following anecdote illustrates the energy-sapping chaos that occurs when we finger-point and blame.

This is a story about four people named Everybody, Somebody, Anybody, and Nobody. There was an important job to be done, and Everybody was sure that Somebody would do it. Anybody could have done it, but Nobody did it. Somebody got angry about that, because it was Everybody's job. Everybody thought that Anybody could do it, but Nobody realized that Everybody wouldn't do it. It ended up that Everybody blamed Somebody when Nobody did what Anybody could have. *(Anonymous)*

Principle Seven
There Is an "I" in Teamwork

"I believe that you control your destiny, that you can be what you want to be. You can also stop and say, 'No, I won't do it, I won't behave this way anymore. I'm lonely and I need people around me—maybe I have to change my methods of behaving,' and then you do it." —Leo Buscaglia

Your interpersonal skills are your greatest asset or liability. You decide.

As we've discussed, one of our signature stories illustrates that most people do not enjoy being around horse manure because of the odor. As you know, manure is a by-product that falls from the horse's rear end. Our seminar participants readily agree that employees prefer to avoid the horse's butt.

The question "Who causes you to be a horse's rear end?" produces interesting answers. Suppose someone throws a cup of water in your face. What would be your reaction? An emotional outburst of anger? Who caused your emotional outburst? The typical answer is the person who threw the water. And that is the wrong answer. You did. When people rain on your parade, you have choices. You could get mad. You could exit. Or, you could control your emotional reaction to learn more about the root cause. Which response did you select? It is imperative for you to accept the responsibility for your behavior that was discussed as Step One of the Seven-Step Personal Change Process from Section One.

We also need to revisit the following behavioral sequence offered by Patterson et al. in their best-selling book, *Crucial Conversations*. As you will recall, there is a natural flow of events leading to your actions. Events occur and immediately you apply an interpretation or create your story. Your story elicits feelings, which in turn result in behaviors.

Experience > Story > Feelings > Actions

In spite of stories generated so instantaneously that they appear out of your control, you can control your response and therefore the ending of the respective story. This is the first way for you to demonstrate the "I" in teamwork. You can exert control to ensure the story is based on facts instead of hearsay or what you think happened. For example, you might think the person who threw water in your face did such to make you mad. In reality, that person may have thought they were assisting you in some fashion. Get the facts!

The second control point is your actions. As we pointed out, you always have options, and getting angry when someone rains on your parade is just one of several. Over the years, we've heard a range of attempts to rationalize inappropriate emotional outbursts, including "I'm just like my mother," "It's in my DNA," "The devil made me do it," "They deserved the wrath of my emotional response," and cultural differences as well.

The point is, you are the "I" in teamwork. The question you must answer every moment throughout every day is, "Am I going to use behaviors to maximize my effectiveness as a leader and therefore my working relationships, or am I going to show people that I'm a horse's butt?"

Principle Eight

Your Perception of Me Is More Important Than My Perception of Me

"Whenever two people meet, there are really six people present. There is each man as he sees himself, each man as the other person sees him, and each man as he really is."

—*William James*

Let's suppose you believe you're dependable, but others don't. Who is right? You are looking at your behavior through the wrong side of the eyeballs; you want to see yourself as others see you. In the figure below, we've modified the Johari Window to show the combinations of what you or others know about you. The following paragraphs provide a summary for each of the four combinations.

Behavioral Awareness

	Known by Self	*Unknown by Self*
Known by Others	Public	Behavioral Blind Spot
Unknown by Others	Mask	Emotional Blind Spot

Public. The desired state is the congruence between what you and what others see. Leaders know who they are. They are confident and comfortable in their skin while constantly striving to improve. Such leaders willingly share their strengths, weaknesses, and personal improvement efforts. They are an open book.

Behavioral Blind Spot. The behavioral blind spot is your reputation that others are discussing—but not with you. In reality, the likelihood is that you will always have a behavioral blind spot, which others may always discuss without you being aware. The danger is that this behavioral blind spot can derail your career. For example, a manager reported that the office manager had been a problematic employee during her entire three years of employment. When asked whether these toxic behaviors had been brought to her attention, her manager stated that he wasn't sure whether anyone in management had ever had the courage to tell this employee about her bad behavior.

Unfortunately, the scenario with the office manager occurs far too frequently in organizations. To avoid this, you

71

must be proactive to learn about yourself and the perception of you held by others. You can do that by being the student who is ready for the teacher to appear by:

- Learning as much about yourself as possible by examining your thoughts, feelings, and behaviors in order to assess your strengths and weaknesses. Why do you think, feel, or respond in particular ways? You must ask the question to obtain the answer.

- Obtaining information from those with whom you work. If you've created the reputation that people can feel free to provide you with verbal feedback, then your supervisor, peers, direct reports, or a friend can provide essential information. If that's not the case, then at least your supervisor should provide feedback. (If not, then that tells a story!) Volunteer to participate in a multi-rater assessment if that option is available to you.

- Taking advantage of self-assessments that are available to you. Teleometrics (www.teleometrics.com) has a comprehensive assessment system regarding your workplace values, using power, sharing and receiving information, and leadership style. The DISC, Johari Window, and Thomas-Kilmann are popular instruments that can provide excellent information about the advantages and disadvantages of your work style. These also help you to understand others.

Being willing to seek the information is only part of the formula. The other parts are accepting and then using the information. In the first leadership principle, Accepting the Brutal Truth, we introduced the three options to receiving feedback. The one you select will tell others the degree to which you are willing to improve and serve as a role model. As a reminder, following are your three choices:

1. Deny that it is true.
2. Believe it, but do nothing about it.
3. Believe it and create the reputation of using the input to improve your interpersonal performance.

We're back to the concept that your body is designed to protect itself from painful events. You must override this temptation in order to take advantage of your third option listed above. Remember, the more painful experiences are rich with learning opportunities. To take advantage of them:

- Understand the importance of needing to know your workplace reputation.
- Create a positive anticipation to learn about your reputation.
- Intellectually and emotionally say, "Whatever I learn is okay." When it is okay with you to receive feedback, you are more relaxed. As a leader, you must learn to accept the brutal truth about every situation, including your performance. Modeling that behavior helps others to do the same.

Mask. Each of us has our mask. For example, think of the last time you showed more self-confidence than you were really experiencing, or being calm when you were emotionally upset. At times, acting can be beneficial.

Pay attention to your masks and then learn whatever is necessary to close the gap between the "real you" and the mask. Let's continue to use self-confidence as an example. If you find yourself constantly wearing this mask, then your brain is telling you that you need to learn more genuine self-confidence. There is only one way to achieve this: the growing experience of stepping out of your comfort zone. (You know how to master this change process, which was detailed back in Section One.)

Emotional Blind Spot. The emotional blind spot can be the most challenging of the awareness elements as it is not easily recognized by you or by others.

We often use the analogy of an iceberg when discussing the two components of our thinking process. The tip of the iceberg constitutes the conscious part of the thinking process, while the large volume of ice hidden below the water constitutes unconscious thought. Content in both levels impacts your behavior. You are the product of a very complex interaction between your genetics and learning history. For whatever reasons, you have placed experiences in your unconscious mind that continue to impact your adult performance.

For example, one young CEO did not trust women and inadvertently considered only male applicants to fill the positions within his senior management staff. To shorten a long story, he became aware that he was extremely angry at his mother, despite that she had been deceased for years. She had never expressed her love for him even though he had provided financial support for her after his father's death. Therefore, he didn't trust women and unconsciously viewed them only as wanting something from him. You can imagine how liberating it was when he discovered this emotional blind spot and how it had impacted his behavior as a leader.

How do you unlock the door to the unconscious to learn more about yourself? One option is to visit with a qualified mental-health specialist. Another option is to study your life's story. Phil McGraw's best-selling book, Self Matters: Creating Your Life from the Inside Out, offers several exercises that can stimulate insightful understanding of adult behavior. The cornerstones of McGraw's exercises include the following:

- Listing the ten defining moments that have helped shape your self-concept and describing how each has impacted you.
- Determining the seven most critical choices you have ever made and how your self-concept has been affected by these choices.
- Identifying the five most influential people in your life and describing their actions and influence they have had upon you.

Use a stream-of-consciousness technique as you write—record your thoughts without filtering or editing them. Your objective is to get the information out of your head. Approach this self-study with the understanding that whatever you learn is "okay"—just open the dam to your mind and let your thoughts gush out.

Learning about yourself and the impact you have upon people is a fascinating journey. Ultimately, you need to decide how to positively impact the lives of those who follow you. Before you finish reading this book, we're going to offer many more suggestions that will help you become the leader people want to follow.

Principle Nine

Everyone is from Missouri—the "Show-Me" State

"Leadership is action, not position."

—*Donald McGannon, broadcasting executive*

As a leader, you're in a glass house with all eyes fixed upon you. Your followers listen to your words, but they believe what they see you do. Everything you do sends a message, and their interpretation of that message (remember our discussions of creating your "story") helps them decide how to respond to you. Whether you like it or not, you're an open book; your behaviors tell people about your values. That's the reality of organizational life. It matters not in which state your organization is located—your people are always from the "Show-Me" State of Missouri. They watch what you do, and your actions speak much more than your words do.

There are three critical questions you must ask yourself regarding your vision, which will be seen by others:

1. What is your personal vision as a leader?
2. What is your purpose as a leader?
3. Do your values support your purpose and vision?

To maximize your effectiveness, model these three elements being aligned as shown below.

VISION

^

PURPOSE

^

VALUES & BEHAVIORS

You want to set the stage for your people to do the same, allowing their values and behaviors to affect their purpose and, in turn, their vision. In the words of best-selling author Rick Warren, "your people will maximize their contributions when living a purpose-driven life."

We will revisit this alignment when we discuss leadership passion.

Principle Ten
Top-Down Change Produces Bottom-Up Commitment

"You must be the change you wish to see in the world."

—*Gandhi*

This chapter's principle is so obvious that traditional change efforts to improve interpersonal performance defy logic. A case in point is the company that spent thousands of dollars providing "soft skills training" (in the words of the training manager) to their first-line supervisors for them to more effectively relate with their employees. When asked what that training included, the training manager did not know, nor could he produce a training manual. What is the likelihood of that training having an organizational impact? At least the company can check "training" off their to-do list, regardless of the cost or the minimal, if any, return on their investment.

We're frequently asked to provide "training classes" to improve the interpersonal performance of down-line managers. The requestor is often stunned when told it's a waste of time, energy, and money to do so. Suppose training is provided to help first-line supervisors improve how they work with their people, which you know is critical for every supervisor. Do you think a long-term behavior change is going to occur if one or more up-line supervisors act like the proverbial horse's butt? The participants may enjoy and want to use the training but will tell you, "It won't work here," adding, "The wrong people are in this training class." Remember, everyone is from the "Show-Me" State.

There is another organizational reality to take into consideration: fish rot from the head down. The point is, when you want your down-line people to act in particular ways, you need to make certain those behaviors are both modeled and supported by the up-line supervisory chain. If not, long-term behavior change is not likely. For example, imagine you want to create an empowering workforce environment, but you've got autocratic up-line supervisors. You know the plausible outcome. This scenario is analogous to the cliché you've heard many times: the weakest link determines the strength of the chain. Remember Byrd's words, "You're either green and growing or ripe and rotting."

The reality is, up-line staff set the performance standards

for their down-line staff. Both the commitment and the desired change to improve interpersonal performance must start at the top and cascade down throughout the company.

Principle Eleven:
Systems Drive Behavior Change

"True teamwork is achieved through alignment and accountability to a shared set of behaviors."

Now that we've established that everyone is from the "Show-Me" State and that top-down change produces bottom-up commitment, it's time to talk about the importance of systems to drive behavioral changes. We introduced this subject in the Introduction to Section One as the rubber band phenomenon; that is, a system is required to keep a stretched rubber band in place, for when you remove the system, the rubber band returns to its original state. As we've pointed out, people react the same, so as you stretch to grow, you need a system to drive the changes or you and your people will regress to the comfort zone via the path of least resistance.

Let's begin by considering the technical side of your business. Changes occur by changing a system and then setting that change template over the affected people. You've gone through enough software conversions and changes to improve production, safety, or quality to have experienced this change phenomenon numerous times. You know exactly what would happen if you stopped using systems to improve safety or the quality of your product or service. There is no such thing as status quo; performance would deteriorate.

Improving people skills within systems is another matter. The need for systems to drive behavioral change is ignored, and instead, the typical procedure is to put people into a training class and hope something sticks. Daniel Goleman, the Emotional Intelligence guru, states that companies waste billions of dollars on training for this reason. At best, only 10 percent of the training sticks.

Let's return to the technical side of your business. As you introduce changes, it is imperative that the following critical components exist:

- You must know your point of origin.
- You must know where you are going.
- You must have a behavioral blueprint and a system to achieve your long-term behavior change.
- Feedback is essential to keep you on track.

In order to achieve these critical components you must:

- Define performance standards so everyone knows what to expect.
- Measure against these performance standards to ensure the performance standards are being achieved.
- Make the necessary adjustments as identified by the data.
- Measure again to ensure the adjustments are getting you where you want to go.

You complete these essential steps every day on the technical side of your business—that's just standard operating procedure. Without the use of these critical processes, your organization would be in complete chaos and doomed to fail.

Since these steps work so successfully for technical success, it's only logical to use them to help improve leadership effectiveness. When working on leadership development, approach it from both an individual and organizational perspective.

Individually, you or other leaders strive to improve your own leadership effectiveness. To assist your change efforts, we introduced the Seven-Step Personal Change system earlier in the book. You may want to review Step Six of that process, which details the personal systems to facilitate your change process.

Organizationally, you don't have the degree of control on the people track that data provide working on the technical track, but you can still implement systems to drive change and leadership effectiveness. You can use data to improve interpersonal performance just as you do to improve technical performance. In Section Three, we will show you the behavioral performance standards for workplace values. We'll refer you to www.teammax.net to learn more about the TeamMax Advantage methodology that uses real-time measurements to quantify interpersonal performance. When visiting that Web site you'll notice an eBook, *Leading Change While Dancing with Resistance,* which applies the Seven-Step Change process to manage the energy systems inherent in the five stages of organizational change.

There are several advantages of using a systems approach to improving interpersonal performance. Systems are empirical and therefore visible. Being visible leads to the following crucial advantages:

- You can hold accountable only what you see; that is, you can hold people accountable to use systems.
- Systems can be modeled and taught.
- Systems can be replicated throughout the organization.
- The use of systems helps maintain long-term behavior changes, which is the absolute goal of every change effort.

Principle Twelve

The Workplace Is the University of Personal Development

"Bury your ego. Don't be the star. Be the star maker!"

—*Bud Hadfield*

Why does your company exist? Traditional answers include to generate a profit for shareholders or to manufacture a product or deliver a service. Obviously these are important, but let's make a paradigm shift. First, though, we want to remind you of the second leadership principle, which states that organizations change when people change. Do you agree with that statement? If so, here comes the paradigm shift: the logical conclusion is that your organization exists to help people develop both their technical and interpersonal skills. The better your people perform, the more successful your organization.

Every day and all day long, you have the opportunity to improve your leadership effectiveness. We encouraged you in Step Six of the Seven-Step Personal Change process to spend time every day in focused practice. That is, at the beginning of the day, decide what must be done to continue your improvement. Evaluate your progress at the end of each day.

One of your most important leadership responsibilities is mentoring and developing your people. As mentioned, you want your people to be better than you because when your people improve, your job becomes easier. You can tell how seriously the leader takes this responsibility by the amount of time he spends coaching. You want to teach your people to capitalize on the opportunity to spend every day in focused practice to improve their technical and people skills.

Section Three
Ten Leadership Values

"Your real performance standards are not the behaviors you expect, but rather the behaviors you accept."

—*BJ Gallagher*

You're an open book. Your leadership behaviors tell followers about you. What do you want them to see? Over the last twenty-plus years, Larry has asked hundreds of employees to identify the ideal leadership values for their company; for example, integrity, trust, and communication. Because values are abstract and open to interpretation, the employees also identified specific behaviors for leaders to and hundreds of behaviors. (This work along with leadership and teamwork strategies is summarized in the *TeamWork Dictionary* written by Larry Cole and Kay Clowney.) This section introduces the ten leadership values and their associated behaviors most frequently identified by employees.

We often use "friendly" as an example of a leadership behavior because it seems so easy to define. If you asked your team members to define the term, you could have as many definitions as you have team members. But let's look back into the technical world. Why doesn't your company allow every leader to define his or her own financial systems, quality control systems, or safety procedures? Because the result would be chaos, and your company probably would not survive. Our position is that the same process should apply to leadership development. Why allow everyone to generate their own definition of friendliness if you truly want to institutionalize friendliness? Sam Walton, founder of Walmart, had his own definition of friendliness that he institutionalized as the "ten-foot rule": employees were expected to thank each patron for shopping at Walmart whenever they were within ten feet of that customer.

Employees have defined friendliness to include the following behaviors.

- Smiling.
- Offering a friendly greeting, such as "good morning," or "thank you for the opportunity to serve you."
- Using people's names when possible.

- Using humor as appropriate—laughter is good medicine.

As you review these behaviors you'll find that:

- Each is empirical; you can observe the behavior being used.
- You can model and teach people to use the behaviors.
- Each behavior constitutes a performance standard; therefore, you can hold people accountable to use that behavior.

The use of each can be measured (using, for example, the TeamMax Advantage methodologies that measure behavior in real time).

Employees find the task to behaviorally define leadership values challenging. They've not previously tried to place behavioral definitions on leadership values. As important as people skills are to attracting and retaining employees, to the overall morale, and to the efficiency of working relationships and thus production, logic dictates that defining leadership values should be a priority within organizations. But it has not been. Typically, organizations don't know how to accomplish this task. Thus, they've traveled the path of least resistance and generally do not even define the leadership values to be institutionalized within their culture. These traditional practices just don't make sense, do they?

Leadership has two dimensions: (1) achieving the

desired results, and (2) developing people. Examining each of these dimensions in terms of a low-intensity and high-intensity factor produces the following configuration.

Leadership Styles

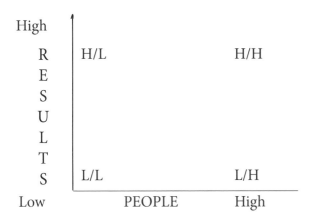

The ideal, of course, is to be the leader who focuses on achieving results while engaging and developing people. The obvious question is whether some leaders have a more natural propensity for ideal leadership than others. Of course some do. The important point is to complete a gap analysis so you know which leadership behaviors you must develop to become this ideal leader. As long as you've got a road map, you can learn essential behaviors. For example, certain personalities find smiling easier than others. But everyone can smile, and each of us can increase the frequency of smiling.

Another example is of a middle manager with an analytical work style who typically went straight to his office upon arriving at work without greeting employees. When he wanted to improve his working relationships with his employees, he began to walk through the department, greeting, smiling, and speaking to employees as he proceeded to his office. This manager will probably remain analytical, but just a friendlier one! Contrast that scenario to the bank CEO who desired to create a more customer-service-friendly environment. When he received feedback that he frequently walked through the hallways without speaking to employees, he agreed but indicated that he was not going to change. The advice offered to him was not an attempt to create a radical organizational change unless he was willing to attempt to change his behavior first. Some leaders don't believe Gandhi's words to "be the change you wish to see in this world."

Communication

"All wise men share one trait in common: the ability to listen."

—*Frank Tyger*

W e're starting our discussion with communication because it's typically labeled the escape goat for many workplace problems. All of us would be rich if we received a dollar for every time we've heard "communication problems" blamed for some mishap in the workplace. We're going to address the two major communication performance standards; however, you'll see communication behaviors throughout the other values as well. Actually, we've already touched on the importance of this issue with the leadership principle be the person that your people will want to talk to; remember, we're communicating all the time through our words and deeds.

Keep people informed with the facts. People want honest communication and information. As simple as that sounds, there are several challenges to doing so. Knowledge is power, but unfortunately, that's the reason some leaders are stingy with the information they share. Their ego gets in the way of effective communication.

We've worked with leaders who despise meetings and prefer to disseminate information to one team member at a time. You know what the one-member-at-a-time methodology produces—confusion. The delivered message is probably not consistent: it can be interpreted differently by team members, and the information is shared rapidly among the team. Rumors then get ahead of the delivery of facts.

Then there are those times when the information cannot be shared. When that happens, be honest with people and tell them that you'll share the information when it is ready to be shared.

Create an environment in which people feel free to state their opinions without fear of reprisal. We've already mentioned that most employees keep silent because of this fear. We hope that's not your desired reputation. There is no way to determine the cost your organization has incurred because someone was fearful to present an idea; let's just say that the cost could have been very high. We're reminded of the story when seven operating room staff members watched in dismay as the surgeon performed an incorrect surgery. Not one employee had the courage to state the error to prevent the mistake. Not good!

The following communication strategies will help create an environment in which people feel free to communicate.

- Develop the reputation of accepting input to improve your performance and that of the organization.
- Recognize that there are no "sacred cows," so your people have permission to discuss any and every issue.
- Remember that your sole purpose is to improve the company's performance, not fulfill your agenda.
- Remain emotionally calm during discussion of sensitive issues. Killing the messenger is never a good idea! Unfortunately, the cemetery is filled with messengers.
- If you really want to push the envelope, put forth an idea and then ask your people to tell you why it is so stupid. The degree to which your people are willing to respond is credence to the fact that they are comfortable to communicate.

In summary, your interpersonal skills create the environment in which people decide the degree to which they can be honest with you. Byrd offers his audiences the following ten rules to help people make the decision to communicate honestly with you.

1. Treat each other with dignity and respect.
2. Praise the accomplishments of each other.
3. Speak kind words to each other.
4. Be encouragers.
5. Seek—and speak—the truth.
6. Focus on what's right; don't worry about who's right.
7. Listen to learn.
8. Smile and have a healthy sense of humor.
9. Do not gossip.
10. Expect excellence in all thoughts, words, and actions.

When considering these individual rules, we must remember that the most important team rule is to hold each other accountable to live the above. To do so, you must practice honesty, which, according to Thomas Jefferson, "is the first chapter in the book of wisdom."

Abraham Lincoln understood this pillar of leadership, as his nickname Honest Abe exemplifies. In addition to his honesty, Abe was influential due to his humility, compassion, courage, determination, and impeccable integrity. Honest Abe knew that if you sleep with dogs, you'll get fleas. He expressed, "Stand by a man when he's right and part from him when he's wrong."

Now that we've got communication under control, let's turn our attention to respect.

Respect

"I suppose leadership at one time meant muscles; but today it means getting along with people."

—*Indira Gandhi*

In our combined 70 years of experience working with people in organizations, the number-one question leaders ask is, "How do I motivate people?" Perhaps the answer has been overcomplicated due to leaders unsuccessfully attempting to bribe or coerce their people using a variety of techniques, because they are unaware that humans are complex beings. We're going to approach this subject of motivation by treating people with dignity and respect.

The short answer to our leadoff question, "How do I motivate people?" is—you can't. Remember from our discussion of creating "my story" that people always have choices. You can't control their choices, but fortunately, there are things you can do to help your employees make the right choices. We've discussed the importance of Step Two and Step Four of the Seven-Step Personal Change Process (Section One) in determining personal motivation levels; that is, the personal benefits accrued have a powerful impact upon motivation levels. One of the greatest benefits employees can receive from you is feeling valued. You do that by respecting them. Effective leaders understand that to earn a "Ph.D." in leadership you must "Preserve Human Dignity."

Care about each employee as a person. Best-selling author John C. Maxwell said it best: "People don't care how much you know until they know how much you care." You show people how much you care in a variety of ways, ranging from the seemingly simple acts of friendly greetings to learning about and discussing more personal issues such as family, exercise routines, and hobbies. There is more to life than work, and you want your employees to obtain a healthy balance of work, family, and personal health.

Another key factor is showing that you care about each employee as an individual as opposed to just another member of a group. We've lost count of the number of employees who have complained that their supervisors don't care about each of them as a person. Whenever that happens, morale takes a major hit, as well as production and profitability.

Ask for input, understand that input, and use it. The psychological bottom line is you're showing people they're important when you solicit and use their input. Contrast that with asking an employee for input while she feels that her input is useless because the final decision has already been made. That's a bummer. When you ask for and use feedback and then publicly communicate the value of such input, morale and performance will soar. These elements are critical to the success of your organization.

We often ask audiences, "How many of you like to be told what to do?" Predictably, the number of hands raised will be few, and the answer depends upon the person's degree of assertiveness. More assertive people like to be in control, while those less assertive prefer to be less risk-taking and more willing to take instruction. Regardless of the assertiveness issue, the recurring complaint is, "There is no use to telling my supervisor anything, because they're going to do it their way anyway." As a leader, that's not the reputation you want—it won't get you to the point where people will want to follow you.

Use your people's specialized knowledge. A smart leader who is people smart will create a psychological environment that unleashes this knowledge. You can begin that process by completing the steps detailed in the preceding paragraphs. You'll complete the process when you have empowered your people to make decisions independent of you. More on the empowerment issue later in this section.

Give credit where credit is due. Two of the most difficult words to say have to be "thank you." The Gallup Organization reports that 65 percent of employees have not received recognition for a job well done in the past twelve months. That's a tragedy. Everyone needs feedback regarding their job performance. This is particularly powerful when recognition is given to an employee for his or her valuable input that improved performance. Providing feedback sends the message that the employee is valued. You want your employees to feel valued for obvious reasons, such as to retain talent, create loyalty, and encourage peak performance.

Now that you've got the critical steps to let your people know they are valued, go forth and show that you value them.

The most meaningful act of appreciation is, and will always be, a handwritten-note. Upon leaving the office of an executive after a business meeting, Byrd met a lady who he thought was the exec's administrative assistant. After introducing himself, Byrd asked what she thought about her manager. She responded, "He is the best leader that I have ever worked for." Byrd's follow-up question was "Why do you feel this way?" She proceeded to open her desk drawer to show Byrd the following handwritten note:

Carrie,

You were a joy every day you showed up. All my best!

Michael

She mentioned that she had not worked with Michael for over three years, and his handwritten note was the only one that she had ever received in her many years of employment with her organization. Leadership lesson: Make someone feel special by sending a handwritten note of appreciation. You can do that by practicing such Random Acts of Recognition Everyday (R.A.R.E).

Trust

"Trust is the lifeblood of relationships."

Now our discussion focuses on the special lubricant of working relationships—trust. Without doubt, trust gives synergy to working relationships. Effective leaders know that trust, once lost, is almost impossible to regain. Fortunately, as with the other values discussed in this section, it is a natural resource, so you can create as much trust as you desire by displaying the behaviors that show you are trustworthy. Let's get to it.

Be dependable. When you tell people you're going to do something, meet or exceed their expectations. It's that simple—under-promise and over-deliver. In those instances when your best-laid plans get off track, let the affected parties know immediately. Keep them informed as to the status of your work.

To help prove they are dependable, effective leaders do the following five things with truth:

They seek it.
They speak it.
They expect it.
They respect it.
They live it.

Keep people informed with the facts. We've addressed this behavior in discussing the communication value. Believing that someone is not sharing all the facts with you is a stimulus that will kick your imagination into high gear, and that's not good. You know the false stories that your imagination can create, so be the leader who prevents your followers' imaginations from creating false scenarios. Otherwise, rumors will get started. To prevent them, keep your people informed with the facts. Communicate, communicate, and then overcommunicate the facts.

Competently complete job responsibilities. All that needs said is that you have to be competent. We've discussed the importance of knowing who you are and accepting the brutal truth about yourself. You need to know your sweet spots and those areas in your life in which you're not so sweet. Knowing this information is important for at least two reasons. One, it will allow you to maximize your strengths. Two, you want team members to be competent in those areas that you're not.

Keep confidential information confidential. You know the importance of keeping confidences. Here's an interesting bit of news: research shows that when you ask people to keep information in confidence, they will most likely tell one person and then ask them to keep it in confidence. You can see the train wreck here. So the best advice is to keep your mouth shut. If you are asked to reveal confidential information, tell the requestor the truth—it is to remain confidential at this time.

Empower. Empowerment is important, and this is the second time it helps drive a value. (Yes, we're going to address it as a separate value to highlight its importance.) People are more apt to trust you when you trust them. We can already hear the "Yes, but . . . ." Your "but" may be that it's extremely difficult for you to let go. If that's the case, then you have a developmental issue. We remind you that you will gain power as you give it away.

The "but" may also be the quality of your team members. If that's the case, then use empowerment as a development tool for them. When empowerment doesn't work, recruit team members who want to become peak performers. Remember that people must be coachable and willing to change. If not, they have made the decision to not be a part of the team.

Be emotionally consistent. It's hard to trust someone who is emotionally inconsistent. Some variations in physical and emotional energy swings are natural, but major mood swings create unhealthy working relationships.

Admit mistakes and limits of knowledge. Honesty shows that you are trustworthy. Readily admitting your mistakes or acknowledging the limits of your knowledge sends the message that you can be trusted to not "pass the buck." All you've got to say is, "I blew that one." Or, "Your good question deserves a good answer, but I don't have the information to answer it," and if possible, follow up to provide that answer.

We've highlighted the basic interpersonal skills of being a trustworthy leader. For a more detailed discussion on this topic, we refer you to Dennis and Michelle Reina's book, *Trust and Betrayal in the Workplace: Building Effective Relationships in Your Organization.*

Teamwork

"Together we can achieve greatness; apart we are doomed to mediocrity."

Along with communication, respect, and trust, teamwork is one of the most important values selected by the organizations we've had the pleasure to work with. You need teamwork to survive as a human being. Think about this as you come up to the next four-way stop sign at a busy intersection: teamwork in this case helps maintain your well-being. It's impossible to calculate the total dollars spent on training events that try to institutionalize the leadership principle of helping others to be successful. Space limitations prevent us from examining reasons the "work" in teamwork often doesn't work. Instead, our focus is to provide a blueprint that will put teamwork to work.

Ensure that employees know what needs to be done to achieve success. It seems a bit trite to have to remind you of this basic fact, but you can't hit a target if you don't know what the target is. We're back to the communication value. Examine the internal customers who depend upon you and your team to meet their needs. Ponder the question, "Do you want to be the weak link in this internal customer chain?" Probably not. It's easy, though, to wrestle with your own alligators and forget the priority of serving your internal customers. Now may be the time to meet with your internal customers to be certain you know what must be done to meet their needs.

Proactively do whatever is necessary to be done. Operate from the principle that "your priority is my priority when you need something from me to achieve your priority." When you see something that needs to be done, do it. Need more be said?

Seek and use feedback. We address this issue in more detail in the next section. For now, the focus is to solicit feedback from your internal customers. Soliciting feedback can range from informal feedback discussions to a more formal internal customer survey. This teamwork behavior speaks to the importance of the leadership principle "be the person with whom others feel free to talk to." The desired teamwork environment is that your internal customers feel free to provide feedback at will.

Blind hogs can't use visual feedback. If we could communicate with the hog so it could use feedback, we could help it find acorns with a great deal of success. Of course, you've got a communication issue with the hog; you want to make certain that your internal customers do not have a communication issue with you. Are frustrations in the working relationship your friend or enemy? The choice is yours. Using feedback to improve teamwork with your internal customers sends the message to them that you are willing to use frustration as your best friend.

Hold team members accountable to achieve the desired results. Even though the implications are that you already do hold team members accountable to achieve the desired result, we thought it best to include it to emphasize its importance.

The morning Larry wrote the first draft of this section, the following quote from Andrew Carnegie appeared in his inbox (and he doesn't believe the correspondence was a coincidence):

"Teamwork is the ability to work together toward a common vision. The ability to direct individual accomplishments toward organizational objectives. It is the fuel that allows common people to attain uncommon results."

Positive Attitude

"Nothing can stop the man with the right mental attitude from achieving his goal; nothing on earth can help the man with the wrong mental attitude."

—*W. W. Ziege*

Employees tell us that a positive attitude is important for two reasons: (1) it helps them feel better, and (2) it is contagious. As to whether a positive attitude is DNA-determined or learned, the results are often mixed. It's a bit depressing to think you might have inherited the non-positive gene and are doomed to a life of negativity. That doesn't sound like much fun. The good news is that you still have a choice. We offer you the following behaviors to encourage you to become a leader with a positive attitude.

Talk about your company's compelling vision. Take advantage of the fact that your people like being a part of something bigger than they are and feeling assured that the company has direction. Imagine being in the ocean in a row-boat without oars. Your destination becomes a victim of the waves, and there's not much of a future in that scenario. You need a vision to get where you need to go.

In a similar fashion, consistently talk about your team's compelling vision and how it aligns with the company's vision. Resist the temptation to get so caught up in the daily struggles that you forget where you are going. Develop the habit of talking optimistically about the success that's helping your team and the company achieve its vision.

Maintain a "can-do" attitude. As Henry Ford stated, there are two kinds of people: those who think they can, and those who think they can't. The problem is they are both right. The journey to success is often 90 percent frustration and disappointment. When you focus on the frustration, you become its victim, and all you will see are the obstacles and not the opportunities. To see the opportunistic 10 percent, you've got to control your attitude by telling yourself, "I will find a way to conquer this challenge." Remember that you find what you are looking for. When you start searching for positive solutions, they will magically appear.

Challenge the status quo. You've got to be pretty good to know that you're not good enough. Show that you're "pretty good" by creating the reputation of continuous improvement. Consistently ask for input on how to improve. Persistently stick to the question until your team is confident they've got the best idea on the table at the time. Be willing to revisit decisions when another idea has surfaced that could possibly improve the previous one. A more formal way to challenge the status quo is to conduct brainstorming sessions that encourage true out-of-the-box thinking. You want all your team's eyeballs looking for opportunities to challenge the "as-is" situation so you can take advantage of the creativity that's been resting within their minds. You're encouraging your team to accept the responsibility to create an epidemic of frustration that will drive the need to change.

Give credit where credit is due, and accept responsibilities for mistakes and failures. This behavior is a tall order. As we've previously mentioned, a recent Gallup poll reported that 65 percent of employees have not received positive recognition for a job well done within the last twelve months! Unless you are one of those old-time thinkers who continually tells us that employees do not need to receive additional recognition for a job they get paid to do, I think you'll agree that we can do better than that. Remember the leadership principle that systems drive behavior changes? Develop a system to recognize at least three team members or internal customers every day. You may have heard the suggestion of starting each day with three coins in your pocket and moving one to the other pocket each time you provide positive recognition.

Another challenge is having the courage to take responsibility for the mishaps that sabotage peak performance. People like to point fingers—we hope this doesn't apply to you. We've heard the following statement many times: "But Larry is the one who messed up, not me! Why should I accept the responsibility?" The answer is simple: you are responsible for everything your people do. So show people that you can take the heat, and accept responsibility for everything that happens with your team. You're going to learn in an upcoming discussion about empowerment, that as a leader you are responsible for whatever happens in your team, so you might as well openly accept responsibility for it. That's something you can't hide from.

Remember that mistakes are learning opportunities. Here's a special opportunity to learn about creating a positive workplace environment. An IBM engineer was called to Tom Watson's office after making a $10,000,000 mistake. Upon learning that the engineer expected to be fired, Watson exclaimed, "Why would we fire you after just spending $10,000,000 to educate you!" That's using mistakes as a learning opportunity.

Be friendly. We've already introduced behaviors that, when practiced, will help you become more friendly. Let's conclude our discussion on being positive with this friendly reminder:

- Smile.
- Offer a friendly greeting, such as "good morning," or "thank you for the opportunity to serve you."
- Use people's names when possible.
- Use humor as appropriate—laughter is good medicine.

Integrity

"When wealth is lost, nothing is lost; when health is lost, something is lost; when character is lost, all is lost."

—*Billy Graham*

Leadership integrity has taken a major hit over the last several years. At the time of writing this book, the public was questioning the integrity of leaders of both British Petroleum and the United States government in light of the oil spill in the Gulf of Mexico.

The value of integrity presents an interesting dilemma; even though many people struggle to define integrity in behavioral terms, they certainly recognize it when seeing someone not demonstrating it. In 2001, the Walker Information Group reported that over 50 percent of employees sampled had witnessed at least one episode of what they considered a breach of integrity within their organization (creatingloyalty.com). Following are the types of episodes and percentage who claimed to have experienced them:

- Lying to supervisors – 26 percent
- Not treating employees fairly – 26 percent
- Improper / personal use of company resources – 21 percent
- Conflicts of interest – 20 percent
- Lying on reports – 18 percent
- Sexual harassment – 18 percent

About two-thirds of the respondents did not report such instances for the following reasons:

- Lacking facts – 35 percent
- Didn't feel the organization would respond – 31 percent
- Didn't know an anonymous/confidential way to report it – 25 percent
- Not their responsibility – 24 percent
- Feared retaliation from management – 22 percent
- Feared being considered a troublemaker – 19 percent

The hundreds of employees we work with often use the

synonyms of honesty and truthfulness to explain integrity. We're going to expand that definition a bit.

Honesty. In *Developing the Leader Within You,* bestselling author John Maxwell writes, "Integrity is not a given factor in everyone's life. It is a result of self-discipline, inner trust, and a decision to be relentlessly honest in all situations." Honesty is demonstrated by presenting the facts—the simple act of telling the truth. This act might not be quite so simple when the truth exposes a mistake you've made. Your body pushes you away from painful events (pleasure-pain principle), but you must override that natural tendency and accept responsibility for your actions. Acting with integrity means no finger-pointing. So if you espouse to be honest, admit your mistakes and limits of your knowledge, keep people informed with the facts, and act in accordance to the values you profess. It's still true—people believe what they see over what they hear, and actions will always trump words. Show your followers they can believe you.

Do the right thing, because it's the right thing to do. According to the *Encarta World English Dictionary,* integrity is the quality of possessing and steadfastly adhering to moral principles or professional standards. Imagine that you're traveling in the wee hours of the morning and come upon a stoplight that shows red. You look around and there is no one watching. Do you do the right thing and stop or just keep driving? If you adhere to the above definition of integrity, of course you stop and wait until it turns green.

Put the interest of the company ahead of individual interests. A recent poll reported that a whopping 60 percent of employees do not trust their leaders to put the interests of the company ahead of their own agenda. That figure hurts. If this number should hold true in your organization, it shows the tremendous challenge you face to show followers you act with integrity.

To demonstrate your intent to put the interest of the company ahead of your personal interests:

- Consistently show how your decisions support the company's vision and purpose.
- Exhibit a willingness to make personal sacrifices to do whatever it takes to help your team and company succeed.
- Always speak positively about the company and other employees instead of yielding to the temptation to engage in trash talk.

Perhaps Max DePree said it best: "Integrity in all things precedes all else. The open demonstration of integrity is essential; followers must be wholeheartedly convinced of their leader's integrity." Simply stated, if people don't trust you, they won't follow.

Accountability

What happens when you put a bit of water in the middle of a strand of uncooked spaghetti? You will soon no longer be able to hold it upright because you've weakened the strength of the strand. That is exactly what happens when accountability is lacking in an organization. Lack of accountability may be the number-one cause for ideas buried in the idea-of-the-month cemetery and for mediocre performance.

Unfortunately, accountability has acquired a negative reputation. Because it is often considered a painful event, most people associate it as a disciplinary process and avoid it like a plague. Let's consider a couple of questions: Do you want your people to be successful? Are your people going to need your assistance from time to time to reach the pinnacle of success? When you offer assistance, you use accountability as a teaching tool. It is the process to help people be successful. So it's really a good thing.

When addressing what accountability entails, you must take into consideration the three responsibilities listed below.

Organizational Responsibility. The primary organizational responsibility is to define the expected performance standards. Most companies do that on the technical side of the business. Conversely, the same companies usually fail to do so when it comes to the people side of the business. Or, if they do, the standards are so vague that the interpretation is left to the whim of the interpreter. That speaks to the very reason we've included Section Three in this book that shows you performance standards that are associated with a select sample of leadership values.

Supervisor Responsibility. Supervisors have several responsibilities.

First, you must talk and walk the talk of the performance standards—"no excuses" is the rule. Whatever you do gives permission for others to act the same. We've heard a countless number of supervisors talk negatively about other departments, yet they expect their people to support those very same departments. See any disconnect in this scenario?

Second, you are a teacher. You might not be an expert in every responsibility area under your level of supervision, but when it comes to leadership, teamwork, managing change, et cetera, you are expected to possess the necessary competence to teach your people.

Third, you must hold people accountable to meet or exceed the defined performance standards. You want to establish an understanding that accepting any performance less than the expected is not an option. Anytime you see performance that is less than expected, recognize the opportunity for a teaching moment.

You should introduce the performance gap in a very socially acceptable manner that will create a safe environment for both you and your employee. Note that the following behaviors constitute a system and can be easily repeated:

- "I need your assistance to help me understand something. You know that overall I am very pleased with your work."
- "What I don't understand is, here's the deliverable I received but I was expecting this . . ."
- "What am I missing here? Did I not communicate effectively? Can you help me understand the difference?"

Personal Responsibility. Imagine what organizational life would be like if everyone followed this simple personal accountability rule: Do what you're supposed to do to meet or exceed expectations. Fortunately, not everyone does that because it creates work opportunities for consultants—just kidding! Back to discussing this serious subject, you must hold yourself accountable to the same high standards that you expect of others.

It's our hope that you will use accountability to achieve synergy among your team members.

Empowerment

"Managers hold on; leaders let go."

Give people power! Okay, so let's do that.
We've already shown you the critical role empowerment plays in showing respect and being trustworthy. As we discuss this value, it's important to remind you that you can empower or give people the authority to act on your behalf, but you are always responsible for their actions; you're responsible for everything your people do.

Delegate authority to make independent decisions. Allowing your people to make decisions independently of you is the essence of empowerment. In doing so though, don't

Empowerment

sacrifice accountability—that's a recipe for disaster. Let's examine the basic empowerment process.

1. ***Agree upon the desired results.*** Note that we said "agree." You want your people to provide input into the final decision for several reasons. First is that it will help them learn to make difficult decisions. Second, you want to consider all the options in order to take advantage of the best one. Third, offering input increases the likelihood of ownership. Ownership entails "we" rather than "I was told to . . . ." Fourth, along with ownership comes higher morale, which leads to higher performance.

2. ***Delegate the degree of authority.*** For a moment, consider a gas tank with markers that show the remaining fuel level. Now consider an "empowerment" gas tank with similar markers. When the employee is fully empowered (marker is on "full"), he has the authority to finalize the most effective way to achieve the desired results. If you ask him to make a recommendation before a "go" or "no-go" decision is made, the empowerment marker might show half full. If you want the employee to present all her options so you know that every option was considered, then perhaps the empowerment marker shows a quarter full. If you want her to explore the options and participate in making the final decision, the empowerment marker probably trends at empty.

In reality, the level of authority delegated depends upon many factors, such as degree of risk, competence level of the employee, and your personal psychological makeup. Whatever level of authority is delegated, be certain it is done without fear of retribution. The last thing you want is your employees constantly looking over their shoulders to see whether you're standing over them with the punishment rod. That would certainly be a morale buster and would adversely affect the quality of the finished product.

3. *Define a time frame.* Not only do you define a time line for the finished product, but you should also schedule several check points. You know what will happen if time lines are not defined—things won't get done efficiently and effectively.

4. *Check the progress level.* The accountability system checks the level of progress as expected per each of the checkpoint time lines. Whenever there is a gap between percent of completion at a given checkpoint, ensure that you hold the employee accountable to provide a logical rationale for the gap and plans to close it at the next checkpoint.

The following two behaviors are not always the most integral components of the delegation process, but we want to bring them to your attention because they are important to empowerment.

1. *Provide employees the opportunity to participate in challenging and meaningful work.* We're very much aware of the debate between the perceived importance of intrinsic motivation and extrinsic motivation. There is one line of thought that the majority of employees simply want to be told what to do, work their eight hours, go home, and be paid every two weeks. We believe that most employees want to be challenged with meaningful work. The research we've completed to examine the impact of this variable reveals that being challenged with meaningful work is a predictor of high morale and retaining talent. Isn't that the outcome you desire?

2. *Provide the opportunity for employees to do what they do best.* The importance of this behavior should be obvious. Enough said.

Fairness

"Though force can protect in emergency, only justice, fairness, consideration and cooperation can finally lead men to the dawn of eternal peace."

—Dwight D. Eisenhower

L et's begin our discussion with a couple of true stories. A young lady was promoted to first-line supervisor from within her work unit. She happened to be good friends with several of her coworkers. After her promotion, morale in the work unit took a major hit, because—you guessed it—other employees thought the new supervisor showed favoritism when she offered morning greetings to her friends before talking to the remainder of the team. Fortunately, that was an easy fix.

In the second story, however, the mistake was not so easy to fix. Members of a team thought their supervisor was really good friends with one of their coworkers. This employee made certain that his colleagues knew about the friendship. His peers thought he was underperforming but felt intimidated and would not discuss these concerns with the supervisor. The sacred cow lived a healthy life for a long time, and the team was doomed to mediocrity.

You will not have respect without equity in accountability. That's the essence of fairness.

Consider the following ways to achieve fairness among your people.

Apply policies and procedures consistently, and hold everyone accountable to the same standard. The frequency that this issue is mentioned within a work unit may surprise you. It seems favoritism is a popular game. Sometimes it is true. Unfortunately, most of the time favoritism is a figment of someone's imagination. But you've got to remember that people see what they expect to see. So if someone expects to see favoritism at work, then favoritism is working. And remember, an employee's perception is his version of reality.

This subject becomes even more critical when relatives are employed throughout the organization. Space limitations prevent further discussion of this subject, but let's just say that if this dynamic is present in your company, work hard to show that policies and procedures are consistently applied regardless of the employees' last names.

Distribute work throughout the team. A favorite complaint by employees is, "I always get the jobs that others don't like." If you've got those types of jobs that you need completed, distribute them throughout the team.

Treat everyone as equal contributors to the team's success. This is a tough one. Not everyone is an equal contributor, and you will like some team members better than others. The situation becomes more complex with the natural tendency to go to the people you know will get the job done. In many instances, we've asked supervisors whether they've tried to coach or teach the underperformer. Sad to say, the most frequent answer is—you guessed it—"no" for a variety of reasons, including it's just faster and easier not to (harkening back to "the path of least resistance enables lower performers"). Remember, it's your responsibility to teach. Help people become better performers, or consider other options if they're not coachable and willing to change.

To help you treat everyone as equal members of the team, reread the behaviors associated with respect.

Continuous Improvement

"On the plains of hesitation bleach the bones of countless millions, who, on the threshold of victory, sat down to wait, and in waiting, died."

—*William Moulton Marston*

You want your team and company to continuously improve its performance record and profitability. Based on our discussion in Section One, organizations change only when people change. The improvement that you desire is predicated on the example you set, because top-down change produces bottom-up commitment. And remember that everyone is from the "Show-Me" State—all eyes are on you.

In his book *The Way We're Working Isn't Working: The Four Forgotten Needs That Energize Great Performance,* Tony Schwartz points out that performance usually gets worse the longer we're in our profession. What's the reason for this sobering news? It's that we often have the false impression that we're good enough. Larry once heard a tennis commentator make the point that "you've got to work hard just to stay where you are." Competition is working hard to improve, and that forces you to do the same or you're left in the competitor's dust. There is no status quo; the moment you decide you're good enough is the moment you start to decline.

Seek feedback to improve your performance. We'll focus on this subject in the next section, but we mention it here because it is critical to performance improvement. We encourage you to reread the leadership behavior of acting in ways so others will feel free to communicate with you. The bottom line is that you should seek feedback from every available source, understand it, and use it to improve your performance and that of your team.

Provide honest feedback to improve performance. You get the opportunity to lead by example, and you receive what you share with others. We hope you're excited about this opportunity to provide feedback and will seek to continuously take advantage of it.

Take advantage of learning opportunities provided by your company. Many times Larry starts a training event by asking for a show of hands of those participants who woke up that morning really excited about attending the training session. You know the number of hands that were excitedly thrust into the air—not many!

As the leader, it's important for you to model a different set of behaviors. Be enthusiastic about the opportunity to attend the learning event. Look for the benefits of participating in the experience and you'll see them—you'll receive what you put into it. After attending the event, discuss the valuable takeaways and how they can be applied within your team or company.

Provide employees learning opportunities through challenging assignments. Challenging on-the-job training opportunities are an excellent way to encourage continuous learning. Keep stretching your people by asking them to step out of their comfort zones.

Use mistakes as learning opportunities. You've read about this behavior in the section addressing how to create a positive workplace environment. It also applies when striving for continuous improvement. We want to introduce you to the After Action Reviews, or "AARs," used by the Army. Upon completing a major task, the team conducts an AAR to identify what they did well and what did not go well. The intent is to learn from both experiences. Most people begin a task intending to do well, not to make mistakes (yes, we know there is a very small percentage of folks who desire to sabotage). Thus, when mistakes occur, you might as well take advantage of them instead of punishing a victim.

Section Four
Managing Conflict

As humans, we tend to make things too complicated. For example, you've got to tell John that his department messed up the order. John always blows up and points his finger. He's not going to like the feedback; he might get angry and will probably blame the sales department for causing the error. To make matters worse, you spend a restless night worrying about John's reaction to the conversation that must take place tomorrow.

It's unfortunate that people's feelings result in them acting "stupidly." This only complicates the need to discuss the situation required to resolve the issue. You've got to deal with the feelings before dealing with the issue.

We have all seen a full range of sabotaging behaviors,

ranging from leaders sticking their heads in the sand and absolutely refusing to deal with conflict, to the bull in the china closet who bullies his way through such discussions. If you examine the following figure, the degree to which those involved share and receive information—both negatively and positively—determines the degree of success of the outcomes.

		Receiver	
		Negative	*Positive*
	Negative	Disaster	Challenge
Sender			
	Positive	Challenge	Ideal

You would think that reasonably intelligent individuals would enter the dialogue to create a win-win environment, one that is best for their company. But as you know, they often don't. These reasonably intelligent individuals lose their common sense and allow themselves to be emotionally out of control. Let's return to the behavioral sequence offered by Patterson et al. that we introduced in Section One.

Experience > Story > Feelings > Actions

As you may recall, there are only two points that you can control. The first is your story. In terms of dealing with conflict effectively, that means talking to yourself so that you remain in emotional control to create a winning solution. The second is your actions. You can control your reactions regardless of your feelings; you do it all the time. Even when you're emotionally charged, you want to use the behaviors to resolve the matter, not make the situation worse. You must control yourself. Remember that right thought is mastery and calmness is power.

Part of the challenge is that the instinctual pleasure-pain response tries to interfere with rational thought. When conflict is viewed as negative, uncomfortable, and even painful, that interpretation triggers the flight-or-fight protective mode. The natural tendency is to avoid or escape the pain through flight, but you must look at differences of opinion as an opportunity to improve the situation at hand. Perhaps it's a teaching moment, a personal improvement opportunity to deal with sensitive situations more effectively or make a decision that will benefit the company. We know that if you look for the good, you will find it. We are not being Pollyannaish; we're asking you to be smart and focus on the benefits of the more pleasurable outcomes.

Many authors have written volumes about conflict management, but in this section, we reduce the subject into bite-size information that, when used, will increase your ability to work effectively with more people in different situations.

Working Differently with Different People

"If you want one year of prosperity, grow grain. If you want ten years of prosperity, grow trees. If you want 100 years of prosperity, grow people."

—*Chinese proverb*

To begin with, we must dispel the notion that the Golden Rule of treating everyone as you would like to be treated is an effective working-relationship principle. Most people do not like to be treated like you do. Instead, you should treat people the way they want to be treated. Tony Alessandra refers to this principle as the Platinum Rule, which is the title of his best-selling book.

By this point in your leadership development, you've probably been introduced to either the popular DISC or the Social Styles (Wilson Learning) personality assessments. If not, Google either one and complete an online assessment. These assessments take a snapshot of your comfort zone on two psychological dimensions, assertiveness and people. Assertiveness represents a willingness to tell people what you think as well as representing an energy dimension. The people dimension represents your willingness to consider other people. Your score will put you into a combination of the following matrix.

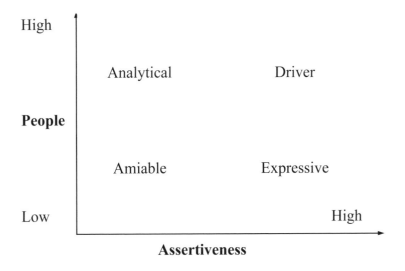

For the purposes of this book, consider Expressives and Drivers as those who are assertive, easily tell people what they think, and have the energy to get things done. Drivers are more results-driven, in-your-face, bottom-line people, while Expressives are more people oriented. On the other hand, Analyticals are very detailed, are procedure oriented, and strive for accuracy. Amiables are the relationship specialists—they enjoy people, and people enjoy them.

Based on our simple descriptions, you can readily see the major differences between the two dimensions, proving that not everyone wants to be treated like you.

In your behavioral repertoire, you display behaviors from all four quadrants. But you have one behavioral set that you rely on, and that behavioral style—Amiable, Expressive, Analytical, or Driver—is your comfort zone. It matters not whether you believe the origin of these behaviors is DNA-based or acquired through your interactions with the environment. The important point is that you choose the behaviors that you show the world.

For a complete understanding of the four work styles represented in the matrix, we refer you to *The Platinum Rule: Discover the Four Basic Business Personalities and How They Can Lead You to Success* or *The Social Styles Handbook: Find Your Comfort Zone and Make People Feel Comfortable with You* by Wilson Learning. We encourage you to continue studying these styles. The more you know about what you are doing to maximize or interfere with the effectiveness of working relationships, the greater the likelihood that you can also manage yourself. For example, both of us are Expressives and quite verbal. At times it is better to keep our mouths closed and actively listen instead of just waiting to respond.

As you complete these personality assessments, you will learn about the other three interpersonal styles and how you can better work with each. For example, you know that Drivers are logical, factual based, bottom-line people who are driven by achieving results. These are not the people to engage in small talk about their families and hobbies, as they likely perceive such discussions as a waste of time and just a way to divert attention from the more important tasks. To maximize your leadership effectiveness and working relationships, knowing the social styles is crucial for building relationships that stand the tests of time and change.

Conflict Resolution

"If you burn the bridges of the past, you'd better be able to walk on water."

We're going to revisit the first figure used in the previous chapter to list the five popular conflict-resolution strategies of the Thomas-Kilmann Conflict Resolution Model. There is more information available about this subject than we can possibly include in this chapter, and we highly encourage you to continue studying this important subject.

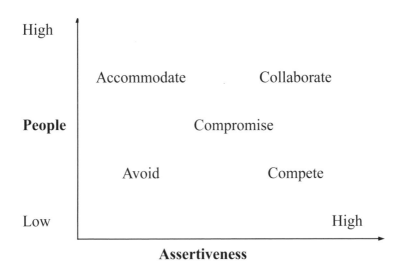

Using this overlay with the figure from Chapter 30 also allows you to examine the interaction among the four work styles and helps create propensity to use these strategies. For example, Drivers are more apt to use the compete strategy, while Amiables are more likely to avoid conflict. However, you will see there is not a 1:1 relationship, so caution must be exercised when discussing the two.

Each strategy has its advantages and disadvantages and can be more appropriate for a given situation than for others. It's all about selecting the right strategy for the right situation. When you take one of the assessments cited in the previous chapter, you'll learn which strategies you tend to underuse or overuse compared to a statistical norm, as well as those that align with the norm.

Overall, collaborate is the ideal because you're working to establish a win-win solution. The collaboration process includes:

- Agreeing upon an overall mutual purpose; for example, "Our purpose is to reach an agreement so our departments work together efficiently."
- Ensuring the facts and needs of the involved parties are clearly defined. Stephen Covey's principle, "first understand, then be understood," can certainly help facilitate this process.
- Brainstorming solutions to meet the stated needs.
- Implementing a solution.
- Evaluating the solution's success and adjusting as necessary.

Staying with the more assertive style is compete. There is no opportunity to provide input when this strategy is employed, because "my way" is the "right way."

As previously mentioned, many leaders rely on the "stick-their-head-in-the-sand approach" to avoid working with different opinions. The difference between avoid and accommodate is that when you compromise, you will work with the diverse opinions rather than run away. When you accommodate you say, "Doing it your way is better, so it's fine with me." When Larry initially completed the Thomas-

Kilmann assessment, he was surprised to learn of his propensity to overuse accommodate in view of his higher assertiveness level.

Finally, compromise occurs when you seek a quick fix. Again, if you're not familiar with the use of these strategies, then put learning about them on your to-do list.

Giving Feedback

"You do not lead by hitting people over the head—that's assault, not leadership."

—*Dwight D. Eisenhower*

The manner in which you introduce a sensitive subject plays a major role in reaching a successful conclusion. Suppose you have an employee who is underperforming, and addressing this problem is long overdue. Let's examine this subject from the viewpoints of the different work styles.

The Analytical approaches the subject in a no-nonsense manner and may rely on the compete strategies. His introduction might sound something like, "Larry, the facts of the situation clearly show that you're not performing at the level to maintain your employment."

The Driver approaches the subject in a similar fashion, also relying on the compete strategy. He might say something like, "Larry, you're just not getting the job done. Either get the job done, or I'll find another person to do it."

Both approaches have the tendency to elicit a negative emotional reaction that could add fuel to the emotional fire. The employee may feel attacked and instinctually, that elicits the fight-or-flight reaction. Neither of these is a desirable option for successfully resolving the performance issue.

The Amiable will want to minimize conflict through avoiding the discussion. He doesn't want to hurt anyone's feelings, unless, that is, he becomes angry and explodes. At that point, it's hard to predict the words about to be spoken! If the Amiable does approach the subject, it might go something like, "Larry, are you aware that at the end of the day you still have a lot of work to get done? I sure wish you would try to get everything done so that no one gets upset over our performance." In reality, the Amiable has excellent interpersonal skills to use in this situation, but his eagerness to avoid conflict interferes with his use of the skills. The Amiable might end up enabling the underperforming employee.

The Expressive may try to approach the subject through humor: "Larry, have you noticed that the more breaks you take, the 'behinder' you become?" Of the four work styles, the Expressive is most likely to approach the subject diplomatically to reach a collaborative decision. The tension of the situation, though, might encourage the Expressive to use sarcastic humor or other similar inappropriate techniques.

Kerry Patterson, Joseph Grenny, Ron McMillan, and Al Switzler introduce a "don't-do" approach in their best-selling book *Crucial Confrontations: Tools for Talking About Broken Promises, Violated Expectations, and Bad Behavior* that can be used regardless of work style or the frequency with which you use conflict-resolution strategies. The objective is to create a "safe" environment, which ties back to the leadership principle discussion in Section Two about helping team members feel free to talk to you. (You might want to reread that principle to refresh your memory.)

Let's begin here by establishing a mutual purpose: "You would agree that it is important for all of us to complete our job responsibilities to help the company achieve our goals, right?" Defining the mutual purpose may take a bit of discussion, but it is an excellent starting point. Once the mutual purpose is established, the use of the "don't-do" introduction sounds like, "The last thing I want to communicate is that I don't value your work, because you can do great work. Now I need you to do more of it." Your objective is to help the employee see the performance gap, so you continue by saying, "You're completing 'x' amount of the needed work, but you need to be completing x + y work. Is that your understanding? If so, can you help me understand the reason the work is not being completed?" We might add that it's not always easy for the underperforming employee to accept responsibility for her performance, so be prepared to present facts, not just what you think or feel.

The objective in providing this feedback to resolve problems is to help the employee feel safe and solicit discussion so you can understand the reasons she is not completing the work. It's possible that you're contributing to the interruption and might not be aware that you're doing so. In that case, you may want to engage the "I am guilty" leadership principle. Ask what you are doing that might be contributing to the underperformance, or what you can do to be of assistance.

Let's close with a bit of humor. When discussing this process during a training session, one of the Drivers in the group exclaimed, "Larry, do you think I'm going to do all of this just to tell the employee that they better improve their performance or they're fired?" The answer to that question depends on how good you want to be as a leader. As we've said, our work style can help or interfere with our leadership effectiveness, and that's the reason you want to know who you are and how you can better relate to others.

Receiving Feedback Differently Because I'm Different

"Feedback is a gift."

P lease don't tell me anything I don't want to hear!"
Living this principle can certainly prevent short-term pain, but in the long run, it can be very painful. Our focus in this chapter is to help you understand how your work style impacts your receiving feedback so that you can take more advantage of feedback that might be uncomfortable but is so crucial for performance improvement. Receiving positive feedback is easy; sometimes you feel a bit awkward, but not nearly as uncomfortable as hearing what you don't like to hear.

An effective leader seeks feedback from every source. She realizes that using feedback is an antecedent to improvement. She understands that she can deny or not use the feedback, but she realizes these two options will get her nowhere and will only set the stage for mediocre performance at best. This leader admits that accolades are nice, but they're not the most beneficial information. She is most interested in knowing what's not working or what needs to happen to be better as a leader and to improve performance within the company. Thus, she understands that the most useful feedback is oftentimes the most painful. So from that standpoint, pain is a good thing! That doesn't sound right, does it?

You're really going to have to override the pleasure-pain principle to become a professional at receiving feedback. We don't know whether anyone gets to the point that they really like receiving feedback that hurts, but you can at least become better at managing your reaction to such news.

The journey begins with understanding the benefits associated with feedback. To prime the pump, we've listed a few. You can certainly add to the list.

First, feedback is critical to get where you want to go. Feedback lets you know where you are relative to where you want to go and serves as a guide to ensure that you arrive at your destination. Getting where you want to go is why you use regular reporting systems to monitor technical performance. We use the TeamMax Advantage to measure interpersonal performance. Do you remember the blind hog example when we discussed the seventh step of the Seven-

Step Personal Change Process? If you could communicate with that hog, it would appreciate specific and immediate feedback that would help him find more acorns. You want to be like that hog!

Second, feedback is essential for long-term behavior change. The reason most people stop trying to change a bad habit is they don't like the feedback—it probably requires too much work for too little gain. Instead of giving up on the goal, perhaps the feedback is telling you that you need a different strategy. Feedback is the backbone for your continuous improvement efforts.

Third is that personally or organizationally, you cannot survive without feedback. Your body asks for water when needed and tells you when to stop drinking. What would happen if one of these feedback systems stopped working? On a related note, you've probably heard examples of the physical damage that occurs when an individual loses the feeling in one of their limbs.

If feedback systems did not exist or were not working properly in your organization, a state of schizophrenia would be the rule rather than the exception. We're sure by now that you understand the critical importance of feedback.

So now that you know the benefits, how do you position yourself to effectively use feedback, especially when it hurts? Let's revisit the social styles. A Driver wants the facts—the bottom line. The Analytical also wants factual feedback. The difference between the two is that the Driver is more likely to accept responsibility, whereas the Analytical tends to rationalize by not having the necessary data or information that he feels is required to make the perfect decision. The harsh facts hurt the Amiable's feelings. Consequently, the Amiable prefers to avoid these feedback conversations and lives by the "see no evil, hear no evil, speak no evil" philosophy. The Expressive has the verbal skills to rationalize the performance. He prefers to look at what caused the problem instead of what he did to contribute to it. Understanding your behavioral dynamics can help you manage yourself in order to maximize the gift of feedback.

Understanding the benefits will help you become more open to painful feedback. Tell yourself that it's okay to get your feelings hurt (Amiables don't like this!); feedback might hurt a bit, but it's not going to kill you. The painful feedback quickly diverts your attention to the hurt. At that point, you make a conscious decision to continue thinking about the pain or start looking for the good. Here is an excellent opportunity to make a good choice by using the Stop & Think technique we discussed during the sixth step of the Seven-Step Personal Change Process. The good choice is to depersonalize the conversation by looking for the benefits, which include the content of the information as well as the ideas generated to improve performance. Focusing on the benefits and engaging in a conversation to understand the feedback redirects your attention from the discomfort.

Now let's consider the flow of this communication sequence.

Immediately upon hearing the information, make a good

choice by understanding that people offer feedback only about what they are interested in. So any feedback tells you the person is interested—that's a good thing. You can even thank her for her interest and for bringing the information to your attention. Engage in the conversation to understand the facts being presented, and then paraphrase to demonstrate your understanding or your intent to understand, rather than defending the "as is" situation. Ask the person for a recommendation to improve performance. (Always ask for a recommendation when someone tells you that something is not working.) This represents another opportunity to engage in a fruitful conversation to achieve your mutual purpose of improving performance. Close the conversation by thanking the participant for her interest and candid feedback, and telling her you look forward to receiving additional feedback regarding the success of the implemented solutions.

Now let's discuss your body language when it comes to feedback. When engaging in conversations that tend to be stressful, your body follows your lead. The antidote is to act calm and in control. No, this is not an oxymoron; follow the blueprint.

- Tell yourself to be calm and in control.
- Assume a comfortable position. Upon doing that, you begin to feel more relaxed and comfortable.
- Use the person's name.

There's one item left to do: put the content of this chapter to work. It's worked for hundreds of leaders, and when practiced, it will work for you.

Section Five

Leadership Topics

We've introduced you to a lot of content that will improve your effectiveness as a leader, but you're not finished—there's more. You now need to learn about the critical role self-awareness plays in your success. We've hinted of the importance of leadership purpose. Now we'll focus on showing you how to develop your purpose and how that contributes to your leadership passion and helps you be more resilient. You'll discover the importance of being resilient and having the energy to keep going in the face of the numerous personal and professional challenges that will attempt to sabotage your life.

The final topics we include here are controlling your ego and being humble.

Self-Awareness

"Whoever knows he is deep, strives for clarity; whoever would like to appear deep to the crowd, strives for obscurity. For the crowd considers anything deep if only it cannot see to the bottom: the crowd is so timid and afraid of going into the water."

—Friedrich Nietzsche

With your eyes closed, ask someone to place an object in your hand. Now feel and describe that object. Your nervous system allows you to be acutely aware of that object and describe it in detail. We wish the psychological nervous system were as easy and provided the same level of detail.

The Stanford Graduate School of Business Advisory Council, consisting of seventy-five leaders, concluded that the number-one challenge for leaders was lack of self-awareness. Self-awareness is a requirement for leaders so they can know who they are. We shared the following figure in Section Two when discussing the leadership principle of accepting the brutal truth. In our examination of the figure, we discovered a major reason for being self-aware and knowing who you are. Not being aware of your incompetence can be the kiss of death to your career.

Awareness and Competency

	Not Competent	*Competent*
Not Aware	Not Aware	Not Aware
	Not Competent	Competent
Aware	Aware	Aware
	Not Competent	Competent

You're good, but you're probably not good in everything. Knowing yourself puts you in the position to maximize your strengths, and it ensures that you've got team members to compensate for your weaknesses.

Several explanations are offered to account for the degree to which you are self-aware. One is that it is a DNA-determined skill. This hypothesis doesn't give those unfortunate souls born with the wrong gene much of a chance. Another premise is that you must experience a major crucible that grabs your attention and helps you realize the importance of taking life seriously. Crucibles can certainly do that, but we don't want you to create one just to prove the point! We believe you can also learn to be more self-aware. Review the behavior change process described in Section One, as the ensuing discussion focuses on Step Six, or the specific behaviors that you can use to increase self-awareness.

You have only two sources of information about yourself: (1) yourself and (2) others. Let's start with you.

You have a history of significant learning experiences of which you may or not be aware. At the risk of being redundant, you must become a student of yourself and consciously examine your thoughts, feelings, and behaviors. Your body is communicating to you all the time; you simply must start listening with an open mind and ask why. The key to opening your mind is your willingness to learn the truth, so accept the insights that appear in your conscious mind. Instead of denying or fighting them, tell yourself it's okay to think about these experiences while asking, "What can I learn about me?"

The chapter on receiving feedback encouraged you to focus on the benefits of receiving information from others. Just as a sponge physically changes shape when it absorbs water, you want to change by absorbing the information shared by others.

Practicing "being in the moment" is an excellent exercise to increase your awareness. Focus on your breathing, how you feel, and what you're doing, seeing, and hearing.

The clutter and noise of life become so dominant that we lose sight of the beauty.

The journey to improve your self-awareness sounds easy enough, but like every behavior change, it requires focused practice. If you are serious about improving your leadership effectiveness, you'll enjoy the journey to increased self-awareness.

Leadership Purpose

"He who wishes to fulfill his mission in the world must be a man of one idea, that is of one great overmastering purpose, overshadowing all his aims, and guiding and controlling his entire life."

—*Julius Bate*

The number of leaders who have not defined their purpose in life may surprise you—it does us.

Several years ago the thing to do was to write and display your company's vision and mission statements. That process quickly acquired a sad reputation, because they simply became ornaments in corporate hallways.

Let's visit Mother Nature for a moment. All of Mother Nature's creations have a purpose or a reason for being. (Granted, we've questioned whether Mother Nature made a few mistakes along the way and created some insects and reptiles that need not be here, but each has a purpose.) Furthermore, each of these creations is being everything it can possibly be, taking into consideration its DNA and physical resources.

Being creatures within Mother Nature's scheme, humans likewise have a purpose and should become everything they can possibly be (taking into consideration the same variables of DNA and available physical resources). Additionally, humans are equipped with the powerful ability to think and reason. Smart people use this powerful information-processing capacity to help develop their potential. This takes us back to Henry Ford's infamous words that those who think they can, can and those who think they can't, can't. Unfortunately, "I can't" thinking consumes many people, and they become victims of their own negative thinking. We've already encouraged you to become an "I can" thinker and put this powerful resource to work. We're again asking you to use this powerful resource to propel your leadership effectiveness by defining your leadership purpose. Larry wrote his first purpose statement twenty-five years ago, which simply stated that he wanted to help people, based on the premise that doing so was what he enjoyed most. That simple statement changed the course of his personal history, became the backbone to develop a consulting career, and laid the foundation for being an author.

An alternate, more comprehensive model is to write your life's story. Review the significant experiences, choices, and people in your life, and record how each contributed to your development. How did these contribute to your values? What do you like and don't like? In the words of Marcia Wieder, "Understand your purpose in life by feeling your heart's desires." As you write and review this document, ask, "Why am I here? What's my purpose in life?" When the student is ready, the answers appear. Once you find the answer, you'll be in a position to enjoy multiple benefits.

1. Your life has a meaning, a reason for being other than taking up space and consuming natural resources. Knowing what it is helps you feel good about yourself, as it removes the confusion of what life is all about.

2. Your purpose offers direction and guidance. Staying true to your purpose automatically rejects being involved in anything that strays away from that purpose. When you say "yes" to your core purpose, you'll say "no" to the things that don't matter.

3. Living your purpose allows you to align your resources to identify opportunities that contribute to fulfilling your mission.

4. Living your purpose gives you staying power, as you will learn more about in the chapter on resiliency.

5. Followers like to follow leaders who confidently

know where they are going. Take the time to discover your core purpose and become the leader who knows where he is going.

Leadership Passion

Passionate hearts committed to a shared vision can accomplish the impossible."

Passion is the fire in your belly. It's a tremendously important intrinsic motivator. You know that as you are endowed with the powerful drives for food, water, safety, and sex. The question is, "Are you passionately endowed to be a leader?" What is the source of leadership passion? Is it based on DNA as some passions surely are? Or is there another source that you can tap into? The following figure answers this question.

Purpose > Passion

Living your purpose puts that fire into your belly. So you can add another benefit to defining and living your core purpose.

Matthew Kelly offers an intriguing suggestion in his best-selling book, *The Rhythm of Life: Living Every Day with Passion and Purpose,* that passion is the product of desires, talents, and needs, as shown in the Venn diagram.

> Passion

Kelly suggests that you can have as much passion as you want if you're willing to put forth the effort to answer a few questions:

- What is your life's story?
- What do your life experiences tell you about you? What are your values? How do you live your values?
- What is your life's purpose? Why are you here?
- What are you good at doing? Enjoy doing? What do you desire or daydream about being? What do you

need in terms of finances, recognition, et cetera? As you answer these questions, you'll become aware that you receive the most enjoyment from using your natural resources and creative talents. So what do you enjoy creating? How does this enjoyment interact with your life's purpose?

One dictionary definition explains passion as "having a keen enthusiasm or intense desire for something." You know yourself better than anyone does (or at least we hope so!); you're a product of your DNA and a complex learning history. Somewhere along life's journey, you received recognition and enjoyment for participating in one of your life's experiences. That episode sparked your interest and passion to be something. For example, Larry was starstruck by invited lecturers and college professors who spoke so effortlessly without the aid of notes. He can remember those experiences as if they were yesterday. He was so inspired that he secretly dreamed of being like them. That spark ultimately led him to be a teacher at the college level. The lure of money led him away from his passion for fifteen years, but he was "rescued" and returned to his passion for teaching after writing his mission statement. Following his life's purpose allows Larry to live his passion by teaching others and tapping into his creative talents. This book is the product of Larry living his core purpose.

We strongly urge you to take the time to complete our suggested exercise for developing your leadership passion.

We think you will ultimately agree that the advantages of doing so will far outweigh any disadvantages. We've listed the following advantages and disadvantages to discovering your passion:

Advantages	*Disadvantages*
More *direction* and a *purpose* in your life.	The time required to think about your life.
A more *meaningful* life.	The mental exertion required.
The *energy* to accomplish what you desire.	Fear of where this process might lead.
The feeling of contributing and making a *difference* in your life.	Learning required to know how to identify your passions.
A better *understanding* about life.	Must change my attitude that "I can" or "I deserve" to live my purpose.
Improved *resiliency*, or "bounce back."	
An overall more *enjoyable* life.	

Resiliency

"We're all going to get knocked down. The question is, will you get up?"

It's often said that it matters not how many times life knocks you down as long as you're willing to get up. Effective leaders get back up. Others become victims of what knocked them down. In the words taken from Catherine Ponder's book *The Dynamic Laws of Prosperity,* those who stand back up realize that "failure is success trying to be born in another way." Those who quit have "accepted the image of defeat," according to Norman Vincent Peale.

What is the difference between the individual Ponder speaks of versus the one Peale speaks of? Genetics is one school of thought: you either have the gene to be resilient or you don't. Sounds a bit fatalistic, doesn't it? The other school of thought is that the number of times an individual gets back up is a product of their learning history. In the words of Byrd, resilient individuals have learned to "not to quit before the blessing."

In the preceding chapter, we hinted that your passion contributes to your resiliency. Now you can add yet another benefit to writing your life's purpose. Examine the following sequence of events.

Purpose > Passion > Commitment > Courage > Perseverance

Living your life's purpose gives you the energy and courage to persevere during the more challenging times. Larry is a classic example of someone who should not have had a successful consulting career. When he founded his company, he did not have a well-defined service to sell, did not know how to sell, and did not have the essential self-confidence to sell successfully, nor was he well financed. But during those trying times when he questioned whether he would make it, knowing that he was living his purpose was the one compelling thought that kept him doing what needed to be done to succeed.

Larry has said many times that success equals 90 percent frustration and disappointment. In case living your purpose isn't a strong enough antidote to help you through the tough times, we've listed additional strategies to strengthen your resiliency.

1. *Take control.* You feel better when you feel in control of your life. That means instead of wallowing in the misery of the situation, start doing what's required to succeed.

2. *Be optimistic.* Look for the good in every situation. How did you benefit from the experience? You learn to be optimistic by being optimistic. Below we've briefly listed the basic components of a system to put more optimism in your life:

- Each night, think of one good reason you want to wake up in the morning.
- Upon waking, be thankful that you've been blessed to wake up.
- Upon waking, spend a few minutes visualizing the kind of person you are going to be that day.
- Wake up at least 30 minutes earlier to spend enjoyable time doing something just for you.
- Complete simple exercises to awaken your body and continue visualizing having a good day.
- Replace the word "problem" with the word "opportunity."
- Act as if you're optimistic.
- Look for the good in everything. You'll find it.

For a more academic discussion of this powerful force, we encourage you to examine William Seligman's works, starting with *Learned Optimism: How to Change Your Mind and Your Life.*

3. Lock onto your goal. Keep your eyes fixed on your goals. Follow the sage advice of a ski instructor who advised Larry and his wife to keep their eyes focused on skiing down the hill instead of focusing on the distractions; your body tends to follow your eyes. Also, your body works to stay in a state of balance, or homeostasis. Tension is created when there is a gap between where you are versus where you want to go. Your brain generates ideas to close the gap and remove the tension. So take advantage of this natural process and trust your brain to be your friend.

4. Maintain a positive attitude. We've spoken to the importance of "I can" thinking. You need those thoughts more than ever, especially when the pain of striving to reach your goal becomes greater than the pleasure associated with the process. If need be, "act as if" you're confident in spite of your feelings. With time, your self-confidence will become more natural.

5. Use feedback. Remember the sage advice that "failure is success trying to be born in another way." Identify what you learned when one of your strategies failed to produce the desired result. You may need to reread the chapter on feedback as a continuing reminder.

6. Change course. Be flexible to change the route to achieving success as directed by your feedback.

7. Have the competence to carry on. Realize the struggle to achieve success is a personal improvement process. That is, you are being given the opportunity to learn both the technical skills and the attitude to be successful. Take advantage of this personal development course—it can literally change your life.

8. Believe in a higher power. People like to feel safe. If you believe a higher power is assisting you on your journey, then that higher power is walking beside you. Your beliefs are your internal reality. A good friend recently shared some advice he was given while facing challenging times: "Trust your business partner. Take action and trust the higher power for things to work for the best."

The words of H. Jackson Brown, best-selling author of *Life's Little Instruction Book,* seem appropriate to close this chapter: "In the confrontation between the stream and the rock, the stream always wins, not through strength, but by perseverance."

Controlling the Ego

Effective leaders understand that big "egos" Edge Greatness Out.

The Chinese symbol for *yin* and *yang* certainly represents the ego. The light side of the ego is the energy source contributing to our positive mental health. We're confident and feel good about ourselves without any need to tell people about our greatness. The dark side of the ego is represented by both ends of a continuum. One end of the continuum represents a poor self-concept and lack of self-confidence. The other end is being overconfident or arrogant. A poor self-concept ("I don't like me") or lack of self-confidence

("I can't") definitely doesn't feel good and often serves as a prison; that is, it keeps us from developing our potential. You don't want to be on the other end and be labeled as arrogant. You might think that feels good, but others certainly won't enjoy being around you.

Both self-confidence and self-esteem are natural resources that you can have as much of as you want. You learn self-confidence by stepping out of the comfort zone and growing to your full potential (detailed in Section One). We've not addressed learning a positive self-esteem, but if you practice the suggestions in this book, you'll develop a more positive self-esteem. Listed below are several suggestions to ensure that your ego is a source of enjoyment. We will then discuss the concept of being humble, which is another way of controlling your ego.

Know your strengths and limitations. Engage in a serious improvement initiative to learn your strengths and limitations. We've encouraged you to learn more about yourself through a self-examination and by writing your life story, discovering your vision and purpose, and consistently obtaining feedback from others. The culmination of this work can help you pinpoint your strengths and limitations. You obviously want to build off your strengths while ensuring that your weaknesses do not sabotage these efforts. Approach the information learned with the attitude that "this could really be me, and it's okay."

Be comfortable in your skin. Be proud of who you are. Enjoy your strengths and openly accept your weaknesses. Be proud of your accomplishments, your vision, and your purpose in life and the goals you are working to achieve. We feel an obligation here to warn you about the dark side of pride (the "yin"): if you wrap your self-esteem around your position, title, or the initials behind your name, you're in trouble. In the words of a medical center CEO to his management staff, "Remember, you were a person before you were titled."

Everyone is equally important. Read the next sentence. Rxmxmbxr that xvxy lxxtxr of thx alphabxt is xqually important to makx a sxntxncx xasily rxad. Like the letters of the alphabet, every person within your company is equally important, regardless of position and title. Learn as much as you can about as many people as you can in your company. We're reminded of a vice-president of a large insurance company who was loved by everyone. Of course, he enjoyed everyone regardless of their position in the company. He carried on a constant stream of communication whenever he walked through the corporate hallways. You can have that reputation as well if you treat everyone with dignity and respect.

Appreciate others. You'll know that you've got your ego in check when you give credit to others for successes, and accept responsibility for mistakes made by your team members. Also remember the truth of the statement that "people don't care how much you know, until they know how much you care." This is an easy assignment: show them that you care. The final suggestion for this topic is to show appreciation of the talents of those around you by empowering them and giving them the chance to do what they do best every day.

Help others be successful. You've seen this suggestion before as a leadership principle in Section Two. The more people you help succeed, the more successful you become. The bonus is that when you help people succeed, it feels really good.

Practice gentleness. Here's an interesting suggestion. Show the "kinder, softer, tender" aspects of your personality. Are you listening, Drivers and Analyticals?

Now that we've got our ego under control, it's time to discuss humility.

Humility

"Humility leads to strength and not to weakness. It is the highest form of self-respect to admit mistakes and to make amends for them."

—*John McCloy*

Here's a challenging assignment for you. Define how you exhibit humility.

That assignment has mystified many participants in our seminars. You might be tempted to include many of the suggestions for controlling your ego that were discussed in the previous chapter. Keep reading.

One of the best discussions on this topic is offered by

David Marcum and Steven Smith in their best-selling book *Egonomics*. If you haven't read it, we encourage you to do so.

By nature, you have an ego. As you mature, you make your ego and, in turn, your ego makes you. You decide your location on this continuum. There is a fine line between being confident and being arrogant. Many confident people appear arrogant from time to time, but you just don't use this label to describe them. It would be nice if a "healthy dose of humility" was genetically "fixed," but that appears not to be the case. Instead, you must learn to be humble, and that produces another challenge: how do you learn to be humble?

A variety of resource materials define humility in terms of "not being arrogant" or "not being boastful." How can you "not be something?" To "not" be something, you must "be" something. To name a few, the reference books speak in terms of being "modest, unpretentious, and respectful." Marcum and Smith offer the following definition: "Humility is intelligent self-respect that keeps us from thinking too much or too little of ourselves. It reminds us how far we have come while at the same time helping us see how far short we are of what we can be." These authors discuss humility in terms of three behavioral characteristics.

1. *We, then me.* Be the person who puts your team and company first and "me" second. That means you are willing to sacrifice yourself for causes greater with no immediate or apparent return to you.

2. *I'm brilliant, and I'm not.* These authors speak to the duality feature of being humble; that is, you are as comfortable being a follower as you are being a leader. Examples of other duality features are listed below:

Strength	Balance
Ambitious	Selfless
Certain	Open-minded
Competitive	Collaborative
Determined	Flexible
Direct	Diplomatic
Intense	Easygoing
Motivated	Patient

3. *One more thing.* Through your competence, you recognize your incompetence. You are a work in progress. In the words of Matthew Kelly, author of *The Rhythm of Life,* "you are becoming the best version of yourself." In this regard, you're managing the gap. That is, you want a high degree of self-awareness of your "as is" situation and want to do what needs to be done to take you to the next level. You want to be in a position to continue maximizing your strengths and minimizing the impact of your weaknesses. Not believing in coincidences, the following quote from Mary Anne Radmacher appeared in one of our inboxes as this chapter was being written: "The jump is

so frightening between where I am and where I want to be . . . because of all I may become I will close my eyes and leap!"

Section Six:
Additional Thoughts
on Leadership

There is so much to tell you that we just had to add Section Six to this book. We thought you might enjoy and benefit from reading messages we have shared with numerous audiences in our speaking on leadership. Each message contains a gem of information that can stimulate additional thought and assist you on your continuing journey to improve your leadership effectiveness. Enjoy!

Do You Pass the Authenticity Test?

"We need to find the courage to say no to the things and people that are not serving us if we want to rediscover ourselves and live our lives with authenticity."

—*Barbara de Angelis*

Subject: Character of Leaders

Our passion and expertise is helping businesses develop authentic leaders whom people want to follow, and our experience has proven that the quality of performance in most organizations is a direct reflection of the quality of leadership. The following four questions help identify the worthiness of leaders:

- Are you competent?
- Do you listen to your conscience?
- Is your character sound?
- Do you have compassion for others?

Research (see *Working with Emotional Intelligence* by Daniel Goleman) has shown that intelligence is not a determining factor in the lives of successful leaders but has proven, if anything, a hindrance. In their pursuit of power and control, many individuals choose to abandon what is right for what is popular. This egotism is truly the "PGA" of the good old boy network: power, greed, and arrogance! Following is what former Enron president Jeffrey Skilling had to say about people at an electricity industry conference in Arizona: "You must cut costs ruthlessly by 50-60 percent. Depopulate. Get rid of people. They gum up the works" (The *Seattle Times,* April 5, 1997).

One of our heroes, Dr. Norman Vincent Peale, made this statement of wisdom that best illustrates what is often missing in today's "bottom-line" business environment: "The softest pillow is a clear conscience."

Because the character of leaders determines the destiny of organizations, we need more men and women who have the courage to stand for what's right and not compromise their souls in the name of political correctness. In their passionate search for acceptance, far too many are busy polishing their personalities at the expense of their character. But personalities are superficial—outward perceptions of what people think—while our character is the true self, who we really are. A Chinese proverb states it best: "If there is righteousness in the heart, there will be beauty in character. If there is beauty in character, there will be harmony in the home. If there is harmony in the home, there will be order in the nation. If there is order in the nation, there will be peace in the world." Wise leaders understand that self-justification is the beginning of self-destruction, and living a life of integrity is simply doing the right thing in all situations, regardless of the consequences.

Finally, and most important, the single greatest responsibility of a leader is to keep hope alive. If you don't love people, you will never lead them. Authentic leaders foster an environment of total trust and understand that to create a sustainable culture of excellence requires the commitment of all team members to a cause greater-than-any-one individual. With rare exceptions, most managers are so possessed with self-promotion they have little time left to serve those they are supposedly leading. As Viktor Frankl, in his wonderful book *Man's Search for Meaning,* stated, "The Statue of Liberty on the East Coast needs to be supplemented by a Statue of Responsibility on the West Coast."

Do you pass the test?

The Power of Words

"Truth spoken without compassion is cruelty."

Our words can soothe a troubled mind or keep someone awake all night.
Our words can heal hurt feelings or break a heart.
Our words can lift a spirit or sink a soul.
Our words can give wings to a dream or ground it forever.

—*Anonymous*

Subject: Words and Communication

Research has proven that words affect every cell of the human body. The most effective leaders filter thoughts through their hearts before they become words. Much too often we let the "venom" slip from our mouths before thinking, letting emotions dominate our intellect. Compassionate leaders, however, have a "Ph.D." in communication; they Preserve Human Dignity.

Watch your thoughts, for they become your words.
Watch your words, for they become your actions.
Watch your actions, for they become your habits.
Watch your habits, for they become your character.
Watch your character, for it is your destiny.

—Anonymous

In conversations, are you most likely to react or respond? Wise leaders stop, listen, and think before they respond. The most important key to effective communication is to ask the right questions, and you will get the right answers. Following is a quiz to assess the degree to which you are an effective communicator.

- Do you typically debate? In ancient Greek, "debate" literally meant "to destroy."
- Do you typically discuss? In ancient Greek, "discuss" literally meant "to tear apart."
- Do you typically dialogue (same as conversation)? "Dialogue" means "a flow of meaning." This is what effective communication is all about—the sharing of meaningful information.

Silence is the most powerful word. Effective communicators understand that "silent" and "listen" contain the same letters. Byrd's mother's words still ring true: "You ain't learning nothing when you're talking!" The most dangerous word: but. Too often we are caught saying, "You did a good job, but . . ." The intended compliment is cancelled by that simple destructive word. When you use but too often, you make a butt out of yourself!

In closing this chapter, we want to share with you ten of the most powerful words you can speak as a leader:

- Four most important: *What do you think?*
- Three most important: *I appreciate you!*
- Two most important: *Thank you!*
- Single most important: *We*

The only way for teams to achieve their full potential is for each member to feel free to share his thoughts, ideas, concerns, and fears. Open and honest communication is, and always will be, the lifeblood of personal and team growth.

Mary Kay on Leadership

"Everyone has an invisible sign hanging from their neck saying, 'Make me feel important.' Never forget this message when working with people."

—*Mary Kay Ash*

Subject: Mary Kay Leadership

I (Byrd) had the pleasure of participating in the 2004 Mary Kay Seminar in Dallas, Texas. I went to sell my new line of motivational gifts but received much more than monetary gain. Throughout the years I have worked with hundreds of companies and thousands of leaders, but after spending eighteen days at the Mary Kay event, I must confess that I had never been exposed to a better business model than the one created by the legendary Mary Kay Ash.

We all know that Mary Kay is a tremendously successful enterprise with quality products that enhance the beauty of women. But in my firsthand observation, the product is not the real power behind Mary Kay. Having spent hours with hundreds of consultants and directors, I am convinced that the heart of Mary Kay's success is the culture that the founder so carefully nourished. Mary Kay was a single parent who worked hard in the corporate world only to be passed over in favor of her male counterparts. She had the vision to imagine a company in which women could follow their dreams and achieve financial success by serving other women.

I asked a very successful Mary Kay national sales director about the Mary Kay culture, and she shared the following response. "I met Mary Kay and asked her what I could do to repay her for what she had done for me." She answered, "Pass it forward." This is the simple force behind the Mary Kay Spirit: women helping women succeed. At Mary Kay, it's not about "me"; it's all about "the power of we."

It was so refreshing to watch and feel the positive energy that occurs when people truly care about each other. In my conversations with these directors and consultants, I found that many had left very successful corporate careers to join Mary Kay. The primary reason is that they felt unappreciated. Corporate America, please take note: it's not all about results!

To truly understand the force that drives this successful enterprise, we need to look no further than what this Dream Company values: God first, family second, career third. Mary Kay understood that success at the expense of faith and family was truly failure, and that a balanced life was the true measure of success. This philosophy is so foreign to the typical business culture that places so much emphasis on performance and productivity, that new Mary Kay consultants have a hard time accepting that this caring culture is truly genuine. One sales director told me that her biggest challenge is helping new consultants understand that caring is more than words at Mary Kay—it's a way of life. She went on to explain that this is such a big challenge because many women come to Mary Kay from environments—both home and the workplace—where they have been shown very little appreciation. It takes time to prove that the Mary Kay Culture—passion for what you do and compassion for those you serve—is real and believable.

For those like me who study winning cultures, this is what I observed to be the four foundations of the successful Mary Kay business model:

- Passion – love what you do.
- Purpose – be a part of something greater than self; the Power of We.
- Preparation – learn something new every day.
- Perseverance – don't quit before the blessing.
- Personal accountability – accept personal responsi-

bility for your life.

It would have been a real treat to have personally met Mary Kay, but I was blessed to feel her spirit through the warm hearts and beautiful smiles of those fortunate to be a part of her family. For that I am grateful.

PS: For those who still feel that winning is everything, you might like to know that 80 percent of the female millionaires in the United States are Mary Kay sales professionals. Success is truly high touch!

The Task of Medicine and Leaders

The task of medicine is to cure sometimes, relieve often and care always."

—Ambroise Paré (1517-1590)

Subject: Caring Words

My mother (Byrd's) was a very simple person, never wanting or wishing for the material things in life. She was a loving wife and mother, fiercely devoted to her family.

One year, fresh out of college and seeking my future in the business world, I received an emergency long-distance phone call while on an out-of-town business trip. It was my dad with news that Mom had suffered a serious heart attack, and that the situation looked very grim, as the attack had destroyed 50 percent of Mom's heart.

The doctor assigned to Mom walked into the cardiac intensive care unit and spoke the following words: "She will be lucky to live one year." Without hesitation, my mother motioned to my dad to come to her bedside. As my dad leaned over, he heard Mom's command, "You fire that doctor!"

Dad dismissed that doctor and a new physician, Dr. Thomas Runge, was selected to care for my Mom. The love and compassion of this new doctor, coupled with total faith in the True Healer, allowed Mom to live thirteen additional, productive years.

Mom's final hospital visit was a special care unit in Houston, Texas. She became very close to one particular nurse, Ms. Edwards, during the final weeks of her life. This lady cared for Mom as a person, not just as a patient. She was kind, caring, and compassionate as she worked with my mother.

The final day of Mom's life, a "code blue" was announced and an emergency team rushed into the cardiac intensive care unit. Ms. Edwards came out and told Dad and me that Mom had died. Through the tears, I asked the nurse if Mom had said anything prior to her death. She said Mom was mumbling, so the nurse leaned over to ask whether she could help. Mom just nodded her head "no" and said her final words, "I'm talking to God," before passing on to heaven.

You know that Ms. Edwards and Dr. Runge would have

been paid the same no matter how they treated my mother. They could have thought of her as "the heart patient in Room 62." But they didn't. They treated her with the compassion that transcends just doing a job. They cared. And in so doing, they had a profound impact on the final days of Mom's life. There is great power in compassion. People don't remember how much you know, but they do remember how much you care.

And you know what? There's room for that in a lot of other places outside the hospital. Compassion, care, kindness, thoughtfulness—they are all needed at your company by your fellow employees. Oh, not if you want to treat it as only a place to go pick up a paycheck. But if you want to be remembered, if you want to make a difference in this life, if you want to make even a small mark in your little corner of the world, show compassion. Then stand back and watch for the miracles!

The question: What is the task of medical professionals, and all leaders? To keep hope alive.

PS: On June 27, 2003, I contacted Dr. Runge to thank him for his care and compassion. During our phone conversation, he made the following statement: "The worst thing a doctor can give a patient is bad news. The truth can be delivered with compassion, thereby keeping hope alive." Beautiful words delivered by a true physician.

The Paralysis of Perfection

"The pursuit of perfection is the most imperfect model."

Subject: Perfection in Leadership

We have found, both in our lives and in coaching others, that perfection is the most imperfect model for life. Perfection is impossible to achieve, and the pursuit of such can cause relationship problems. Those driven by the addiction of perfection are never pleased with their lot in life and have a hard time understanding others who aren't as driven.

One of our favorite books on self-improvement is *The Four Agreements: A Practical Guide to Personal Freedom.*

In this enlightening book, Don Miguel Ruiz shares the following agreements that were embraced by the Native Americans:

- Make sure your words are impeccable.
- Don't assume anything.
- Don't take anything personally.
- Always do your best.

Agreement Number Four, "Always Do Your Best," is another way of describing excellence; when we continually strive to be our best and not focus on pleasing others and comparing ourselves to others, we will achieve great peace and fulfillment. We also wanted to share Mr. Ruiz's powerful insights on perfectionism:

"The more self-love we have, the less we will experience self-abuse. Self-abuse comes from self-rejection, and self-rejection comes from having an image of what it means to be perfect and never measuring up to that ideal. Our image of perfection is the reason we reject ourselves the way we are, and why we don't accept others the way they are."

Winston Churchill, one of the world's most well-known leaders, said that "The maxim 'nothing but perfection' may be spelled 'paralysis.'"

Live your life, the only life you can live, the life you were born to live. That's good enough.

Conclusion

In closing, we would like you to reflect on the following words written by an Anglican bishop in the eleventh century, which were found in the crypts of Westminster Abbey:

"When I was young and free my imagination had no limits, I dreamed of changing the world. As I grew older and wiser, I discovered the world would not change, so I shortened my sights somewhat and decided to change only my country. But it, too, seemed immovable. As I grew in my twilight years, in one last desperate attempt, I settled for changing only my family, those closest to me, but alas, they would have none of it. And now as I lie on my death-bed, I suddenly realized: If I had only changed myself first, then by example I would have changed my family. From their inspiration and encouragement, I would then have been able to better my country and, who knows, I may have even changed my world."

Looking in the mirror of truth is good advice. One of the basic truths in life is that the only one you can change is you, and by changing yourself, you have the greatest impact on others. Quit trying to "fix" others, and instead, work on being the best you can be. It requires the least amount of energy and is the most cost-effective investment that you will ever make.

Always remember that leadership is all about building relationships that stand the tests of time and change. As we stated in the introduction, every organization has both a technical and people rail, and it's the people rail that propels the organization to true sustainable growth and profitability. To reinforce that point, we would like to share the following Leadership Success Formula:

$$TC + PC = LC$$

Technical Competence + People Competence = Leadership Competence

It's our hope that the insights in this book will help you become the leader people want to follow. Who knows, you might even change the world!

Appendix:
Bonus Leadership Insights

NATURAL LAWS OF LIFE

🌑 **Law of Association:** Show me your friends and I'll show you your future.

🌑 **Law of Appreciation:** The number one desire of people is to be appreciated.

🌑 **Law of Discipline:** Simple acts of daily discipline are the catalyst to growth.

🌑 **Law of Authenticity:** You can only be yourself, so be your best!

WINNING TEAMS ...

Trust each other
Respect each other
Understand each other
Enjoy each other

©2008 True Growth Associates

Three Levels of Leadership

- Level 1: When people understand you, you get their attention.
- Level 2: When people trust you, you earn their loyalty.
- Level 3: When people know you really care, you catch their hearts.

If you don't love people, you will never lead them.

Managers Hold On; Leaders Let Go: Why People Control

1. Lack of trust.
2. Lack of confidence.
3. Low self-esteem. "I feel better about me when I control you" attitude.

4. Ego/arrogance. "I'm better than you" attitude.
5. Perfectionism. "Nobody can do it better than me, so I'll do it myself" attitude. Major reason for burnout.

Caution: The harder you hold onto people and things, the more apt you are to lose them.

Five Questions That Help Assess the Health of Your Organization's Culture

1. How healthy is your culture? Beware of your blind spots, as what you don't know that you don't know will keep you from developing as a leader.
2. Are associates treated with dignity and respect?
3. Is management trustworthy?
4. Are opinions both solicited and valued?
5. Is there equity in accountability (same standards from entry level to executive level)?
6. Do people feel appreciated?

Facts of Life

- What you resist persists.
- New habits often occur when the pain of staying the same becomes greater than the pain of change.
- Change is inevitable but growth is optional.
- The winds of change will either blow you away or take you to new heights.

Recommended Reading

Abrashoff, D. Michael. *It's Your Ship: Management Techniques from the Best Damn Ship in the Navy.* Business Plus, 2002.

Baggett, Byrd. *Can You Trust Me? Simple Insights on How To Live and Lead with Integrity.* True Growth, 2009.

Baggett, Byrd. *Dare to Lead: Proven Principles of Effective Leadership.* Cumberland House Publishing, 2004.

Bennis, Warren, and Burt Nanus. *Leaders: Strategies for Taking Charge.* Harper Paperbacks; 2nd ed., 2003.

Blanchard, Ken. *The Servant Leader.* Thomas Nelson, 2003.

Buckingham, Marcus, and Curt Coffman. *First, Break All the Rules: What the World's Greatest Managers Do Differently.* Simon & Schuster, 1999.

Buckingham, Marcus, and Donald O. Clifton. *Now, Discover Your Strengths.* Free Press, 2001.

Byrum, C. Stephen, and Leland Kaiser. *Spirit for Greatness: Spiritual Dimensions of Organizations and Their Leadership.* Littleton, MA: Tapestry Press, 2004.

Clifton, Donald O., and Paula Nelson Dell. *Soar with Your Strengths: A Simple Yet Revolutionary Philosophy of Business and Management.* 1995.

Cole, Larry, and Michael Cole. *People Smart Leaders: Maximizing People, Performance, and Profits.* Oakhill Press, 2004.

Collins, Jim. *Good to Great: Why Some Companies Make the Leap . . . and Others Don't.* HarperBusiness, 2001.

Cottrell, David. *Leadership Energy (E=mc2): A High-Velocity Formula to Energize Your Team, Customers and Profits.* CornerStone Leadership Institute, 2008.

Ibid. *Monday Morning Leadership: 8 Mentoring Sessions You Can't Afford to Miss.*Cornerstone Leadership Institute, 2002.

DePree, Max. *Leadership Is an Art.* Crown Business, 2004.

Gerstner, Louis V. *Who Says Elephants Can't Dance?: Leading a Great Enterprise through Dramatic Change.* Harper Paperbacks, 2003.

Gladwell, Malcolm. *The Tipping Point: How Little Things Can Make a Big Difference.* Back Bay Books, 2002.

Jaworski, Joseph. *Synchronicity: The Inner Path of Leadership.* Berrett-Koehler Publishers, 1996.

Marcum, David, and Steven Smith. *Egonomics: What Makes Ego Our Greatest Asset (or Most Expensive Liability).* Fireside, 2008.

Maxwell, John C. *The 360 Degree Leader: Developing Your Influence from Anywhere in the Organization.* Thomas Nelson, 2006.

Moore, Harold G., and Joseph L. Galloway. *We Were Soldiers Once and Young: Ia Drang—the Battle That Changed the War in Vietnam.* Presidio Press, 2004.

Morris, Tom. *If Aristotle Ran General Motors.* Holt Paperbacks, 1998.

Ibid. *If Harry Potter Ran General Electric: Leadership Wisdom from the World of the Wizards.* Crown Business, 2006.

Murray Bethel, Sheila. *A New Breed of Leader: 8 Leadership Qualities That Matter Most in the Real World.* Berkley Trade, 2009.

Myrer, Anton. *Once an Eagle.* Harper Paperbacks, 2002.

Phillips, Donald T. *Lincoln on Leadership: Executive Strategies for Tough Times.* Warner Books, 1993.

Rath, Tom, and Donald O. Clifton. *How Full Is Your Bucket? Positive Strategies for Work and Life.* Gallup Press, 2004.

Rath, Tom, and Barry Conchie. *Strengths-Based Leadership.* Gallup Press, 2009.

Sample, Steven. *The Contrarian's Guide to Leadership.* Jossey-Bass, 2003.

Shaara, Michael. *The Killer Angels: The Classic Novel of the Civil War.* Ballantine Books, 1996.

The Social Styles Handbook: Find Your Comfort Zone and Make People Feel Comfortable with You. Wilson Learning Nova Vista Publishing, 2004.

Staub, Robert E., II. *The Heart of Leadership: 12 Practices of Courageous Leaders*. Staub Leadership Consultants, 2007.